We Can't Go Home Again

We Can't Go Home Again

AN ARGUMENT ABOUT AFROCENTRISM

Clarence E. Walker

OXFORD
UNIVERSITY PRESS

2001

OXFORD
UNIVERSITY PRESS

Oxford   New York
Athens   Auckland   Bangkok   Bogotá   Buenos Aires   Calcutta
Cape Town   Chennai   Dar es Salaam   Delhi   Florence   Hong Kong   Istanbul
Karachi   Kuala Lumpur   Madrid   Melbourne   Mexico City   Mumbai   Nairobi
Paris   São Paulo   Shanghai   Singapore   Taipei   Tokyo   Toronto   Warsaw

and associated companies in
Berlin   Ibadan

Copyright © 2001 by Clarence E. Walker

Published by Oxford University Press, Inc.
198 Madison Avenue, New York, New York 10016

Oxford is a registered trademark of Oxford University Press

Library of Congress Cataloging-in-Publication Data is available

ISBN 0-19-509571-5

Book design & composition by Mark McGarry
Set in the Scala family of types

9 8 7 6 5 4 3 2 1

Printed in the United States of America
on acid-free paper

*For Paul Goodman, professor of history,
and Jacquelyn Mitchell, director of
African-American studies*

Men make their own history, but they do not make it just as they please; they do not make it under circumstances chosen by themselves, but under circumstances directly encountered, given, and transmitted from the past. The tradition of all the dead generations weighs like a nightmare on the brain of the living. And just when they seem engaged in revolutionizing themselves and things, in creating something that has never yet existed, precisely in such periods of revolutionary crisis they anxiously conjure up the spirits of the past to their service and borrow from them names, battle cries, and costumes in order to present the new scene of world history in this time-honored disguise and this borrowed language."

Karl Marx,
THE EIGHTEENTH BRUMAIRE *of Louis Bonaparte*

. . . when you give Negroes the facts in their case, they call for flattery and misinformation.

Carter G. Woodson

When all men think alike, no one thinks very much.

Walter Lippman

CONTENTS

ACKNOWLEDGMENTS

In the course of writing and researching this book I have incurred a number of debts. As an American historian, I am fortunate to have a wide circle of friends in both the United States and abroad. In the course of preparing this book I was able to present my work at the Universities of California at Berkeley, Davis, and Irvine; Amherst College; Carleton College; University of Charleston; John Hopkins University; University of Illinois Urbana–Champaign; Northwestern University; University of Oregon; Oregon State University; University of Tennessee, Knoxville; and Wesleyan University, Middletown, Connecticut. I also gave lectures at the Universities of Düsseldorf, Glasgow, Hamburg, and Manchester, venues where I presented chapters of this monograph. The following scholars made my visits rewarding and intellectually challenging: Herwig and Bettina Friedle, Rudi Keller, Simon Miller, Nikos Papastergiadis, and Shelia Rowbotham.

Over the course of the past twenty-five years I have made some very good friends who share my love of history. Although I no longer teach at Wesleyan University, I still have a wide circle of friends there. Since 1973 Henry Abelove has been a close friend, an intellectual mentor, and a first rate critic of my work. Similar debts of gratitude are owed to Erness and Nathan Brody, Anne DuCille, Harris Friedberg, Patricia Hill, Marylin Katz, Mel McCombie, Gail Pemberton, Clair Potter, Joseph and Kit Reed, Iris and Richard Slotkin, Andrew Szegedy-Mazak, Ann Wightman, and Janice Willis.

When travelling on the East Coast I could not survive without the hospitality and friendship of Rosalind, Jerry, Cliff, Kim, and Nicholas Rosenberg, who have provided me with a home when I am away from California. Among my California circle, Bruce Poch, Dean and Vice President of Admissions of Pomona College, has been for more than fifteen years a friend who has cooked with me and discussed the culture of American colleges and universities, while we turned out sumptious Thanksgiving meals and BBQs during the summer. I owe him and two former members of his staff who took an interest in this project, Chris Hammett and Jason McGill, a debt of thanks. Although they do not live or teach in California, Daniel and Valinda Littlefield contributed a great deal to the completion of this book. Both Bruce Dain and Suzanne Marchand sent me materials that helped shape my argument and broaden my understanding of the origins of Afrocentrism. I should like to thank them for their assistance.

The University of California system has been a most hospitable place to work. I would like to thank my colleagues Emily Albu, Lindon Barrett, David Biale, Cynthia Brantley, Martha

ACKNOWLEDGMENTS

Bowsky, Joan Cadden, Steve Deyle, Joanne Diehl, Bill Hagan, Karen Halttunen, Deborah Harkness, Catherine Kudlick, Mike Mahony, Clarence Major, Barbara Metcalf, Abdulh Jan Mohamed, Jacob Olupona, Ruth Rosen, Mike Saler, Ronald Saufly, Seth R. Schine, Valerie Smith, Stylianos Spyridakis, Blake Stimson, Alan Taylor, Patricia Turner, Georges Van Den Abbeele, David Van Leer, and Louis and Spring Warren, who answered numerous queries about areas of history and culture outside my expertise. This project could not have been completed without the aid and support of some of my past and present graduate and undergraduate students: James Brooks, David Del Testa, Kathleen Du Val, Lawrence W. Goldstein, Theodore A. Hamm, Keith Heningberg, George Jarrett, John Logan, Frank Malarete, Kenneth Miller, Seth Rockman, Carl Sjovold, Rosa Maria Tanghetti, and Brian Teeter.

Finally, the manuscript was read and criticized incisively by the following historians: Robert Abzug, David Blight, Edmund L. Drago, Thelma Foote, Kevin Grant, Michael Johnson, Waldo Martin, James Oakes, Rosalind Rosenberg, Nick Salvatore, Daryl Scott, John Sweet, F. B. Tipton Jr., and Robin Walz. No historian could ask for a better group of friends. We do not at all times agree about things historical but differences about the interpretation of the past enrich our friendship. I would like to thank them all for putting up with my intellectual high jinks. At a crucial moment in my work the eminent Byzantinist Speros Vryonis, Jr. Director of the Speros B. Vyronis Center for the Study of Hellenism invited me to give a talk, and he and his staff were very gracious in their criticism of my work. I should also like to thank Professor Vyronis former Assistant Professor Stelios Vasilakis for his help with some of the Ancient history materials. I also want to thank both Kate Gilbert and Kathleen Van Der Meer for teaching me the importance of commas, and Natalie Karst, who typed many versions of the manuscript. My thanks also go to Stephen Auerbach who was an excellent proofreader. Finally, special word of thanks is owed to my editor at Oxford University Press, Peter Ginna, who waited patiently for the book to be completed.

NOTE ON USAGE

Throughout the text I use the terms *Negro* and *black* interchangeably. I am uncomfortable with the term *African American,* and one of my purposes in writing this book is to show why.

INTRODUCTION

This little book is an intervention in the debates about Afrocentrism. It offers a critique of the focus in Afrocentric discourse on Egypt (called Kemet) both as a black civilization and as the progenitor of Western civilization. In making this argument, I readily acknowledge that Afrocentrism is a popular form of black cultural nationalism.[1] What this text does is raise questions about Afrocentrism as a form of historical consciousness. Although some of its advocates may claim that Afrocentrism is history, the methods by which its proponents reach their conclusions are not historically rigorous. The scholars who call themselves Afrocentrists have not written history in the strictest sense of the term; what they have produced is a therapeutic mythology designed to restore the self-esteem of black Americans by creating a past that never was. Concocting for themselves and their followers a mix of historical notions and views, Afrocentrists use a historical style of

argument to validate their analysis of the cultural plight of contemporary black Americans.

What is Afrocentrism? According to Molefi K. Asante, the leading Afrocentric spokesman in the United States today, "The Afrocentrist seeks to uncover and use codes, paradigms, symbols,
motifs, myths, and circles of discussion that reinforce the centrality of African ideals and values as a valid frame of reference for
acquiring and examining data. Such a method appears to go
beyond western history in order to revalorize the African place in
the interpretation of Africans, continental and diasporan."[2]
Asante does not use the word "history" in this quotation, but a
curious amalgam of historical fact and fiction nevertheless occupies a central place in his and other Afrocentric scholars' work.[3]
Asante's call for studies of the black past that "revalorize the place
of Africans" is echoed by Maulana Karenga when he says the primary goal of black studies is the "rescue and reconstruction of
Black humanity."[4] When placed in the context of Afrocentric writing, these statements have another meaning, since Asante and
Karenga are saying that black Americans are psychologically dis-
armed in the face of whiteness. According to Asante, black people,
in order to be healed, have to be placed in "the middle of their
own historical context as active historical agents."[5] To attain a
proper sense of historical awareness, blacks in the United States
must "begin from where [they] are" by studying "African-American
history and mythology." Studying these subjects will lead Negroes
to conclude that their understanding of the black past is not only
incomplete but false. The remedy for this state of historical false
consciousness is Afrocentricity.[6] "Afrocentricity is the centerpiece

of human regeneration," according to Asante.[7] Devoid of both "ideology" and "heritage," black people are like ants "trying to move a large piece of garbage [who] find that it will not move."[8] The answer to this state of inertia and deracination, in which black Americans are confused by a "discontinuous history and an uncertain future," is Afrocentrism.[9] Operating as a form of cultural recuperation, Afrocentrism heals and restores black psyches wounded and disoriented by centuries of Eurocentric historical presumption and arrogance. Afrocentrism contests the claim that Greece was the progenitor of Western civilization by assigning this role to ancient Egypt. "The Afrocentric analysis," says Asante, "reestablishes the centrality of the Ancient Kemetic (Egyptian) civilization and the Nile Valley cultural complex as points of reference for an African perspective in much the same way as Greece and Rome serve as reference points for the western world."[10] Underlying these claims that Kemet, not Greece, is the mother/father of the West is the belief that black people's true history has been stolen from them. Professor Amos N. Wilson, a psychologist, calls this "the theft of history." He goes on to say, "We, in studying Egyptology, are trying to take back what European historiography has stolen, completely falsified; to erase the new false identities it placed on the Afrikan Egyptian people."[11] A similar line of argument is presented in one of the most influential Afrocentric texts, George G. M. James's *Stolen Legacy*.[12] The false identity or idea that these texts attempt to correct is the notion that black people have historically been ciphers in world history. If what I call here Egyptian (Kemetic) Afrocentrism has one task, it is to correct the idea that Europe was/is the source of all knowledge and black people have historically been hewers of wood and drawers of water. In *Stolen Legacy* James writes, "Consequently, the book is an attempt to show that the true authors of Greek philosophy were not the Greeks; but the people of North Africa, commonly called the Egyptians; and the praise and honour falsely given to the Greeks for centuries belong to the people of North Africa, and therefore to the African Continent. Consequently this theft of the African legacy by the Greeks led to the erroneous world opinion that the African Continent has made no contribution to civilization, and that its people are naturally backward."[13] James does not use the term "Kemet," but others writing in the Afrocentric tradition do.[14] The use to which some Afrocentrists have put this term is instructive.

The ancient Egyptians called the desert *deshret* (red land) "to distinguish it from the fertile *Kemet* (black land), so called because of the black soil that was deposited along the banks of the Nile by the annual inundation."[15] Within the ancient world the Egyptians called themselves *remetch en Kemet* (the people of the black land).[16] In a similar vein, Americans call both the Black Hills of South Dakota and the black belts of the South "black," not in reference to the people who live there but to the color of the soil. In Afrocentric scholarship, however, the word "Kemet" has been translated to mean "land of the blacks." Within Afrocentric scholarship, this translation of Kemet as "land of the blacks" is clearly an ideological move. Egypt (Africa) is constructed as the source of civilization—the place from which Europe (Greece) derived its mathematics, science, philosophy, and art. The emphasis on Egypt thus has a racist subtext, since black displaces white as the progenitor of Western civilization. In short, Afrocentrism reverses the Manichean dualism in which white is the sign of all that is good, creative, and valuable, and black is the mark of evil and incompetence. Rather than transcend the racialism of nineteenth-century Aryanism, Afrocentrism only repeats it. If Afrocentrism had remained purely a black cultural nationalist "thang" and had not become entangled in the culture wars— specifically, those concerned with the teaching of Western civilization—it would not have become the subject of public and scholarly debate. But the publication of Martin Bernal's controversial work *Black Athena* (1987) was seized upon by the Afrocentrists as proof that they were correct in their claims about the origins of Western civilization. Bernal's enormous tome argues that Egyptian and Semitic cultural influences shaped the formation of Greek civilization. Bernal does not say that the Greek goddess Athena was black or that the ancient Egyptians were black:

> To what "race" did the Ancient Egyptians belong? I am very dubious of the utility of the concept "race" in general because it is impossible to achieve any anatomical precision on the subject. Moreover, even if one accepts it for the sake of argument, I am even more skeptical about the possibility of finding an answer in this particular case. Research on the question usually reveals far more about the predispositions of the researcher than about the question itself. Nevertheless, I am convinced that, for at least 7000 years, the population of Egypt has contained African, South West Asian and Mediterranean types. It is also clear that the further South, or up the Nile one

goes, the blacker and more Negroid the population becomes and that this has been the case for some time.[17]

Later on, however, Bernal makes the curious statement that he thinks the pharaohs of the First, Eleventh, Twelfth, and Eighteenth Dynasties were rulers "whom one can usefully call black."[18] But what does it mean to say that people can "usefully" be thought of as black or, for that matter, any color? The utility of this analytical strategy escapes me. Not surprisingly, the relationship of Egypt to Greece has been the subject of spirited discussion in both classics and African-American studies departments in American colleges and universities.[19] In California, where I live and teach, the Egyptian school of Afrocentrism is popular on the campuses of both the California State University system and the University of California.

In addition to creating a stir in the academy, Afrocentrism has also stimulated debate in the public schools. The power of Afrocentrism can be seen in its ability to shape school curricula in cities as diverse as New York; Columbus, Ohio; Oakland, California; Portland, Oregon; Sacramento, California; and Washington, D.C. In 1988 Professors Wade W. Nobles and Lawford L. Goddard submitted to the California Department of Education a proposal for sex education in the Grant Union High School District in Sacramento, California. The project, aimed at ninth-grade black males, was intended "to change their attitudes toward sex and reduce teenage pregnancies."[20] Called "Hawk" (high achievement, wisdom, and knowledge), the project was based "on the Philosophy, Culture and Values of African and African-American People."[21] Employing a methodology that was described as "culturally consistent," the authors of the Hawk project promised to transform "behavioral dysfunctioning resulting from unmet human needs."[22] In fact, the effort to raise black student self-esteem informs all Afrocentric education projects. In Columbus, Ohio, for example, in June 1993, a teacher in the Columbus public schools asked the school board to establish an Afrocentric alternative school for black students, a suggestion that was discussed in the pages of the *Columbus Dispatch* for several years, from June 1993 to July 1997. One advocate of the plan emphasized the need for black students to "learn about their own heritage so that they can have some positive people to emulate other than basketball and football players."[23] In Washington, D.C., a similar type of program aimed at boosting the self-esteem of black students was introduced in 1994.[24] I will have more to say about the emphasis on self-esteem in Afrocentric discourse shortly.

I have chosen to explore Egyptian (Kemetic) Afrocentrism because it is the most popular and powerful expression of this enthusiasm currently sweeping black America. Afrocentrism's popularity can be understood as part of a broader process of change in black America that, for lack of a better term, I will call "communityism." A turn to communityism is not bad in itself because community has played an important role in the process of American social mobility. It is clear that members of white ethnic groups made their move up the American social ladder as communities and not as individuals. For example, many Jewish New Yorkers worked together to elect Herbert Lehman, the first Jewish person to sit in the U.S. Senate. In Boston, Irish Americans did the same thing for the Kennedys. Both of these ethnic groups created strong institutions to help their members move up the social ladder, acquire wealth, and establish a political position in American society.[25] Black people did the same when they elected Oscar DePriest to Congress in 1928 and Adam Clayton Powell Jr. in 1944.[26] Community in this sense is good, purposeful, and empowering. What is wrong with this current vogue of communityism in black America is not community per se, but Afrocentrist and other black nationalist racial essentialism, hostility to difference, and authoritarianism. I take particular exception to the Afrocentrist claim that black people who disagree with them are either "insane" or somehow not black.[27]

I am especially disturbed by Afrocentrism because of its dangerous political implications. I do not agree with the historian Wilson J. Moses, who has argued that Afrocentrism is a "quaint folksy cultural tradition."[28] If Moses means by "quaint" and "folksy" that Afrocentrism can be understood as only a set of benign folk beliefs, he is wrong. Afrocentrism may at one time have been innocent and devoid of political ramifications, but this is not the case today. On the contrary, within the context of contemporary black political and cultural politics, Afrocentrism constitutes a form of totalitarian groupthink. This can be seen most clearly when Afrocentrism is placed in the context of communityism. As a central component of communityism, Afrocentrism calls for the creation of a new black psychology based on a positive African-centered history. This process of "recentering" is intended to place American Negroes (called Africans) "in the center of [their] own historical contexts as subjects not as objects."[29] This is an admirable project, but was there ever a people who became agents (actors in the historical process) who were not at one time dependents? In arguing that black people have been so oppressed that they have become "objects" rather than "subjects" of history, the Afrocentrists overstate their case. No oppressed people is ever totally socialized by its oppressor because even within the most oppressive social structures, the subalterns retain a significant measure of control over their lives. In black American history this can be seen in the historiography of slavery—which the Afrocentrists seem to consider embarrassing or unimportant. But they should not ignore it, since historians of slavery have, for almost a century, been working on precisely the issues of agency, identity, and culture that preoccupy the Afrocentrists.

Since the 1950s, the historiography of slavery has moved away from U. B. Phillips's plantation school model of slave socialization to a more complex and nuanced analysis of how North American slaves created a space for themselves on southern plantations.[30] The failure of Afrocentric discourse to deal with changing historical interpretations is related to Afrocentrism's obsession with the therapeutic. Afrocentrism's emphasis on the psychological rehabilitation of black Americans ignores the structural barriers American Negroes have faced historically in the United States.

The inability of Afrocentrism to grapple with the structural derives from the fact that it is a vulgar form of identity politics. In its call to black Americans to "recenter" themselves in "Africanity," Afrocentrism rests on the dubious assumption "that no one can know anything beyond their own bodily identity." Blackness in Afrocentrism operates as the sole arbiter of cognition; because of this, there can be no universal understanding of the past (or, for that matter, of anything) because "truth," "understanding," and "knowledge" are racial, or group specific.[31] Operating within this weltanschauung, a racialized subject becomes liberated from the hegemonic force that oppresses him or her. The Afrocentrists, like the Victorian politician and writer Benjamin Disraeli, think "all is race. There is no other truth."[32]

Afrocentrism's focus on race and psychology mirrors the right wing's critiques of black culture found in the recent work of Abigail and Stephan Thernstrom and Dinesh D'Souza. Although these strident voices emanate from the right, their conclusions about black Americans are remarkably similar to those of the Afrocentrists.[33] Both offer psychological explanations for the continuing difficulties of blacks in twenty-first-century America. What white conservatives and Afrocentrists share is a common conviction that American Negroes lack the "right stuff"—a positive mental framework and culture of achievement.

For Afrocentrists, this problem manifests itself in what Molefi K. Asante calls "mentacide," or "suicide of the minds."[34] According to Asante, Afrocentrism is the vehicle of cultural recuperation for deracinated black Americans living outside of their historic African culture. For the right, the problem is framed in terms of blacks failing to internalize the ideology of bourgeois uplift. Having been coddled by the federal government and liberal paternalism, they claim, Negroes must learn to "root hog or die," as it was argued in the nineteenth century.[35] For both groups the issue is not structure but mind. When viewed as an exercise in "mind cure or new thought," Afrocentrism is neither radical nor contestatory.[36]

Afrocentrism is in some ways a modern recapitulation of Booker T. Washington's accommodationism. Like Washington's program, it deemphasizes politics. In addition, Afrocentrism is an expression of decline, just as Washington's ascendancy signaled black political, economic, and social decline in the last quarter of the nineteenth century. Currently in the United States, the Supreme Court's ban on racial redistricting suggests that electoral politics is a limited strategy for black empowerment. The problem of black congressional representation is also complicated by the fact that in seven years Negroes will no longer be the nation's largest racial minority. In 2005 the U.S. Latino population will outnumber that of black Americans. The growing assertiveness of other American racialized subjects (Asians, Native Americans, etc.) and the increasing size of many of these groups is likely to mean that black people will stop being the focus of the country's racial concerns in this century. Although this changed state of racial affairs will have a profound effect on black American politics and life generally, Afrocentrism has neither answers nor a program for dealing with it.

To compensate for blacks' expulsion from the political sphere during his era, Booker T. Washington preached the ideology of self-help.[37] "The Wizard," as Washington was called, urged Negroes to become achievers and to think positively, believing that this would impress whites and provide blacks with an avenue to social and political equality. The widespread racist violence, both physical and psychological, that black people suffered in the last quarter of the nineteenth century is but one indication of the problematic nature of Washington's analysis of the race problem. Like Washington's plan for black uplift, Afrocentrism confuses culture with politics.

Although culture and politics are related in many ways, they are nonetheless distinguishable. Cultural belonging, black Americans quickly learned after the Civil War, did not confer political belonging.[38] As a strategy for black liberation, Afrocentrism assumes, as Washington did, that black people will be more respected if they have a purposeful and positive culture. For American white supremacists in both the nineteenth and twentieth centuries, however, the problem with black people has never been their culture but rather their very presence in American society.[39]

Why is Afrocentrism so popular among certain sectors of middle- and lower-class black America? The popularity of both Afrocentrism and communityism can be explained in terms of political factors within and beyond black America. In both cases, the situation is grim. With the election of Ronald Reagan in 1980, the federal government's commitment to racial equality regressed toward the racial laissez-faire policies of the last quarter of the nineteenth century. Although Afrocentrism predates the Reagan ascendancy, it is, in part, a particular response to this changed state of political/racial affairs: an accommodation. In other words, contemporary American race relations, if not exactly repeating an earlier pattern, are at least being influenced by earlier modes of racial interaction. This withdrawal from politics into culture also explains the popularity of communityism at this particular moment in black American history. Perceiving a weakened government commitment to civil rights, some Negro Americans have given additional emphasis to a Booker T. Washington–style ethos of self-help. Naturally, a number of black academics, working in both integrated and historically black institutions of higher learning, have been quite happy to seize on this language of community for their own self-aggrandizement. This troubling situation raises the question, Why do people give these scholars what Hannah Arendt forty years ago labeled "unending infallibility"?[40]

It is in this context that Afrocentrism operates as a form of what Karl Mannheim named "utopian mentality," a mind-set he described "as being incongruous with the state of reality within which it occurs."[41] As an exercise in cultural recuperation or recentering, Afrocentrism urges American blacks to re-embed themselves in the cultures of ancient Egypt and precolonial Africa. The black community is asked to embrace what Mannheim called "conceptions of life," ideologies that are "transcendent or unreal because their contents can never be realized in the societies in which they exist, and because one [cannot] live and act according to them within the limits of the existing social order."[42] Yet black people in the United States live in a postindustrial social order and cannot revert to or recreate what A. N. Wilson, writing in another context, has characterized as "the ethics and values of a vanished age."[43] Not only is this impractical, it is also undesirable and dangerous. As mythologies go, Afrocentricity is bad because it is not politically capacitating.[44]

All people need myths to sustain them—through moments of travail and through good times. But these mythologies should be both complex and grounded. Afrocentrism offers not an empowering understanding of black Americans' past but a pastiche of "alien traditions" held together by simplistic fantasies. This is what Afrocentrism does when it claims Africa as the ur-site of Western civilization.

When placed in the broad context of nationalism or racial romanticism, Afrocentrism is neither original nor exceptional. On the contrary, it fits into a pattern of historical fabrication that cuts across racial and ethnic lines. Indeed, the ideas preached by the Afrocentrists derive, for the most part, from Europe rather than Africa. The following passage, if the word "African" were substituted for "European" and "African" for "Aryan," could have been written by Molefi K. Asante, John H. Clarke, Yosef Ben-Jochannan, or the Maulana Karenga. It was, in fact, composed by the Englishman William E. Hearn in 1879.

That family of nations of which I write is confessedly the foremost in the world. It includes almost all the nations of Europe. It includes the Empire, once so great, of Persia, and the multitudinous tribes of Hindostan. Its history is more glorious, its renown is more diffused, its progress in science and in art is more advanced, its religion is more pure, its politics and its laws are more beneficent and more just, than those which prevail elsewhere upon earth. It, too, is that great mother of men by whose sons vast continents have been, and still are being, won from the wildness of nature, and converted to purposes of human use and human enjoyment. By their strong arms and their bold hearts the aspiration of Poseidon has been fulfilled, and the Aryan name and the Aryan fame have been borne wherever Eos sheds her rays. The early history of such a race is worth an inquiry for itself. Except, therefore, when it is necessary to prove the present existence of some social force which has ceased to operate among ourselves, I have omitted all notice of non-Aryan peoples.[45]

Hearn's proclamation of Aryancentrism contains the same preposterous claims as Afrocentrism. The major difference between these two "isms" is power. Hearn's racist observation was made during the nineteenth century, when Europe tightened its grip on Africa and Asia, and was part of what Edward Said has called the "culture of imperialism." Europe could do this because of the technological and military superiority it was able to deploy against societies lacking similar tools of conquest. Afrocentrism's appeal, on the other hand, lies in the cultural production of a mystical blackness, which accompanies the contemporary emphasis on community. Black Americans should not allow themselves to be gulled by this debilitating form of racial politics.

If my readers have concluded from what they have read so far that I doubt the claim that there can be no "objective knowledge about the past,"[46] they should understand that I think some historical explanations are more compelling than others. Like most historians, I do not assume that historical writing constitutes an *absolute* truth about the past—only a *probable* truth.[47] Following rules of evidence, this work is a critique of Afrocentrism that raises questions about its truth claims. It is currently fashionable in both academic and nonacademic circles to deny the validity of truth claims, on the grounds that we can never really know the past because history is "incapable of establishing any real facts about the past."[48] This line of argument, for example, enables revisionists to deny the Holocaust and to say that slavery did not cause the Civil War.[49] I think these claims are intellectually, morally, and politically bankrupt.

Hannah Arendt understood this problem when she wrote, "To this aversion of the intellectual elite for official historiography, to its conviction that history, which was a forgery anyway, might as well be the playground of crackpots, must be added the terrible, demoralizing fascination in the possibility that gigantic lies and monstrous falsehoods can eventually be established as unquestioned facts, that man may be free to change his own past at will, and that the difference between truth and falsehood may cease to be objective and become a mere matter of power and cleverness, of pressure and infinite repetition."[50] Arendt knew nothing about Afrocentrism, but in this passage she captures the limitations of that movement and other exercises in irresponsible historical revisionism. In parts 1–2 of this volume I explore the origins of Afrocentrism and contextualize the movement in contemporary American race relations.[51]

Since I take on not only Afrocentrism but the writing of black history and history in general, I situate my work in the tradition of critical history, what Friedrich Nietzsche described as "history that judges and condemns."[52] Specifically, my scholarship is contextualized in a tradition of black discourse that I call the "black self-critical." This form of writing, which dates from the late eighteenth century, makes its initial appearance in the work of the

Reverend Richard Allen, the first bishop of the African Methodist Episcopal Church. Before the Civil War, this type of discourse flourished in articles and books written by Martin R. Delany and Frederick Douglass and after the war in the work of T. Thomas Fortune, Booker T. Washington, W. E. B. Du Bois, Ida B. Wells, and Anna Julia Cooper. In the early twentieth century, the tradition was kept alive by Du Bois, Marcus Garvey, Kelly Miller, and George Schuyler. But most important for my work were four books I read as a teenager: Ralph Ellison's *Invisible Man*, E. Franklin Frazier's *Black Bourgeoisie*, J. Saunders Redding's *On Being Negro in America*, and Richard Wright's *Black Boy*. All of these books are critical reflections on the question of black subjectivity. They explore the ironic, tragic, and comedic aspects of being black in the United States. The black intellectuals who wrote them were critics of both Negro life and American society. They were not racial romantics, and their refusal to subscribe to certain racial orthodoxies made them outsiders within black America. The lesson I learned from their work was to think critically about both the past and present of black people. Richard Wright captured the essence of the "black self-critical" when, commenting on his disagreements with his black peers in the Communist Party, he observed that he was more interested in "questions" and his comrades in "answers."

I think my readers should know something about my educational background. I grew up in an integrated, working-class neighborhood in West Berkeley, California, between 1944 and 1957, when my father died. When I say integrated, I mean my family was the first black family to own a home on our block, although there were other black families in the area. Negroes were a minority in this section of West Berkeley until the 1950s. Growing up in a racially mixed environment and attending Columbus Elementary, Burbank Junior High School, and Berkeley High had a profound impact on how I think about the world. Long before it became fashionable in American society to style oneself as an integrationist, I had learned to be receptive to a wide range of ethnic and racial differences. In short, my elementary and secondary education was a major factor in shaping both my intellectual and my racial sensibilities. This process continued during my undergraduate and graduate education. I was never attracted to black nationalism in any of its separatist or racially essentialist forms. Like Frederick Douglass, I believe in the black protest tradition, which emphasizes racial inclusion rather than separation. Both my life and my formal education have led me to this conclusion. I also value this education because it was the genesis of my intellectual curiosity, aggressiveness, and contempt for the banal.

A number of the black kids I grew up with—Shirley Brooks, Marlene Moody, Samuel Stansberry, and others—did not think that demonstrating their intelligence in school was a form of racial inauthenticity or "acting white." To read a book, answer a question in class, or in general show you were intellectually competitive was not thought of as an act of racial betrayal. Our integrated education in fact served the function of racial and intellectual demystification; that is, we did not think of particular people or groups as being smarter than others.

At Columbus Elementary School, I played with Negro, Chinese, Japanese, Irish, Italian, Jewish, Norwegian, and Mexican-

American children. In this environment it was clear that no racial or ethnic group had a monopoly on intelligence, since in my classes there was a wide range of intellectual abilities that cut across racial, ethnic, and gender lines. My chief competitor for best reader in Ms. McCarthy's fifth-grade class was a Chinese-American student named Suzanne Fong. Suzanne regularly outscored me on the state diagnostic test for reading. There were others who also outperformed me in primary grades. The result of this education was not a withdrawal into fantasies about blackness. I wanted to experience the world in its fullness and not become solipsistic. I therefore could never be an Afrocentrist or any other type of "centrist." My loyalty is to my friends, regardless of their color or gender or any other part of their identity. I have, moreover, never believed in what Toni Morrison has called "undiscriminating racial unity."[53] In my life I have learned that the late associate justice of the Supreme Court Thurgood Marshall was correct when he said "that there [is] no difference between a white and black snake, they both bite."[54]

| PART ONE |

If Everybody Was a King, Who Built the Pyramids?

Afrocentrism and Black American History

Afrocentrism is a mythology that is racist, reactionary, and essentially therapeutic. It suggests that nothing important has happened in black history since the time of the pharaohs and thus trivializes the history of black Americans. Afrocentrism places an emphasis on Egypt that is, to put it bluntly, absurd. Furthermore, Afrocentrism caricatures Africa by homogenizing the diverse experiences of Africans across both time and place. Finally, Afrocentrism does not, as one of its leading proponents asserts, constitute "a new historiography founded on African aspirations, visions and concepts."[1]

When you strip Afrocentricity of its claims to being a form of historical revisionism that restructures "language to tell the truth,"[2] it falls short of being a constructive approach to history. For history to be credible, it must be grounded in data, and it should relate the local and particular to the macro or general. Good history should give its actors agency, show the contingency of events, and examine the deployment of power. It should also seek to understand its subjects on their own terms. Afrocentrism fulfills none of these criteria and therefore should be read as another "selective rendering of history," in the tradition of nationalist movements since the nineteenth century.[3]

In fact, how could it be otherwise, since Afrocentrism is Eurocentrism in blackface? This can be seen in the very categories Afrocentrism uses to define itself. Frequently used words such as "classical" and "African," for example, have a Western etymology and are not African in origin. The word "classical" comes from the Latin adjective *classicus*, which originally referred to someone belonging to the highest of the five classes of Roman citizens.[4] Later on, according to Seth R. Schein, the word "classical" was applied to the Greek and Roman languages to distinguish them from modern Romance languages, which were viewed by linguistic purists as corruptions of Greek and Latin.[5] As for the word "African," this too derives from Europe.[6] People living in the classical world thought there were several Africas: the "north face of Africa along the Mediterranean coast, the 'Black Africa' to the south, and especially the connection via the Nile through Nubia to the Sudan that formed also a 'third Africa.'"[7] When Molefi K. Asante calls his new textbook *Classical Africa,* which Africa is he referring to? In using this terminology, Asante and the other Afrocentrists get conscripted into the very categories they claim to be contesting.[8]

Similar problems arise with the word "Europe." In the first place, there was no conception of a place called Europe in the ancient world.[9] Only in the thirteenth and fourteenth centuries did the idea of Europe emerge, closely tied to the concept of Latin

4

Christendom.[10] In fact, the word "Christendom" preceded the use of the word "Europe."[11] People living on the European continent between the tenth and fourteenth centuries defined themselves as either Latin Christians or Orthodox Christians. The enemy of both groups was Islam. Between 950 and 1350 Latin Christendom moved east, conquering and colonizing lands that were not considered civilized. These territories, by the fourteenth century, called themselves "Europe."[12] Thus, like "Africa," "Europe" was an invention, and the idea of Europe, as Gerard Delanty has noted, was "connected to state…tradition and elite cultures rather than with the politics of civil society."[13] Delanty then goes on to observe the fluctuating meaning of "Europe."

> To speak of Europe as an "invention" is to stress the ways in which it has been constructed in a historical process; it is to emphasise that Europe is less the subject of history than its product and what we call Europe is, in fact, a historically fabricated reality of ever-changing forms and dynamics. Most of Europe is only retrospectively European and has been invented in the image of a distorted modernity. Moreover, the history of Europe is the history not only of its unifying ideas, but also of its divisions and frontiers, both internal and external.[14]

Thus the meaning of what has been called "Europe" or "European," like the meaning of "Africa" and "African," has been contested transhistorically—a nuance that is lost on the Afrocentrists along with the fact that the very term itself, again like "African" and also "classical," is of European origin.

I take issue with a number of Afrocentrists who claim that Africa—particularly Egypt—was the mother of the West.[15] This assertion is questionable first of all because most cultures are hybrids rather than the omnicompetent entities that Afrocentrists would have us think they are. For example, ancient Egyptian architecture and writing resulted when the Nile Valley civilization came in contact with the Sumerians.[16] Irrigation, the lifeblood of the land of the pharaohs, also developed out of Egypt's contacts with Sumeria.[17] These examples of cultural borrowing are important because they illuminate another of the Afrocentrist historians' major failures—their emphasis on origins. Afrocentrism is a textbook example of what the French economist Francois Simiand called "the chronological idol, that is, the habit of losing oneself in studies of origin."[18] But focusing on "origin" or "who did what first" reveals very little about the past. I will address this problem below.

Despite the claims of Afrocentrism to be new, it is not. Celebration of either Ethiopia or Egypt as a place of black origin and achievement is many centuries old. A positive image of Ethiopia emerged in Europe during the Middle Ages. Latin Christians thought that they would someday be joined in their struggle against Islam by Christian Ethiopia, which was ruled by a mythical king named Prester John.[19] Another source for the belief in Africa as agent of redemption and accomplishment was an "obscure passage in Psalms 68:31 which prophesied that 'Princes shall come out of Egypt; Ethiopia shall soon stretch forth her hands unto God.'"[20] As a child I read this passage on paper fans in my grandmother's church in Sugar Land, Texas. Grandmother could not tell me why princes were coming from Egypt and

Ethiopia and not from other parts of the Biblical world. I found the answer to my childhood question when I became a historian, however. According to James Campbell, after the King James Version of the Bible was published, the word "Ethiopia" came to be used "as a generic term for Africa."[21]

Afrocentrism draws on the tradition of viewing Africa, or "Ethiopia," in the broader sense, as a site of black accomplishment. Historians call this idea "Ethiopianism," and in the nineteenth century both black Africans and black Americans used Psalm 68:31 to give themselves a historical past of accomplishment. According to Campbell, in the nineteenth century the term "Ethiopia" "possessed both a literal reference to contemporary Abyssinia, the one African state not yet under colonial rule; and a metaphorical one, existing outside historical time. In practice the references shaded into one another."[22] What Campbell has written about the nineteenth-century African proponents of Ethiopianism is equally true of today's Afrocentrist. "In invoking Abyssinia," he notes, black Africans "laid claim to a thousand-year Christian history that belied the notion of a uniformly barbarous African past; indeed the presence of a Christian kingdom in Africa at a time when Europe was sunk in paganism inverted colonial history, portraying Africa as the true cradle of civilization."[23] Afrocentrism draws on the spirit of this tradition, but in a de-Christianized form.

The idea that black Africans could play a role in Christianity's triumph over Islam faded after the Crusades. This notion became untenable as that section of the world we now call Europe became involved in the sixteenth century in selling black heathens to the New World. What did not die, however, was the notion that Africa was the original site of civilization. This belief was kept alive in the next century by the Freemasons, who, following Herodotus, regarded Egypt as the source of knowledge. This bit of Masonic esoterica had a profound impact on black thought in the eighteenth century, especially on those blacks who became Freemasons themselves.

Freemasonry developed in seventeenth-century Scotland, became popular generally in Europe in the eighteenth century, and thereafter spread to North America. In the wake of the Revolutionary War free Negroes led by Prince Hall, who had fought in the war, founded their own lodges because they were excluded from white Masonry. The first black Masonic lodge was organized in Boston in 1775. Adopting the name Prince Hall in 1787, it developed after 1791 into a national black fraternal organization.[24] The importance of an African genesis for Masonry was proclaimed without qualification in Martin R. Delany's 1853 treatise, *The Origins and Objects of Ancient Freemasonry*. "Truly," Delany wrote, "if the African race have no legitimate claims to Masonry, then it is legitimate to all the rest of mankind....It is a settled and acknowledged fact, conceded by all intelligent writers and speakers, that to Africa is the world indebted for its knowledge of the mysteries of Ancient Freemasonry. Had Moses or the Israelites never lived in Africa, the mysteries of the wise men of the East never would have been handed down to us."[25] Later Delany observed:

> Was it not Africa that gave birth to Euclid, the master geometrician of the world? and was it not in consequence of a twenty-five

8

year residence in Africa that the great Pythagoras was enabled
to discover that the key problem—the forty-seventh problem of
Euclid—without which Masonry, would be incomplete? Must I
hesitate to tell the world that, as applied to Masonry, the word—
Eureka—was first explained in Africa? But—there! I have
revealed the Masonic secret, and must stop![26]

These ideas became part of the tradition of black Masonry, pass-
ing into the culture of the black middle class and later influencing
Afrocentrism. As I discuss below, these ideas were also part of the
abolitionist vindication of black people.

During the last quarter of the eighteenth century, the idea that
Africa had been the original site of civilization was given a new
impetus in Europe. Looking back to the ancient world, French
savants plotted the growth of civilization from the Nile Valley to
Greece and Rome.[27] In 1796, the philosopher Constantin François
de Chasseboeuf, later given the title of Compte de Volney by
Napoleon, published a book that was to have a profound effect on
black and white abolitionists in Europe and America. *The Ruins:
Or, a Survey of the Revolutions of Empires* was based on de Volney's
travels in Egypt and Syria. Writing about the Middle East, de Volney observed, "It was there that a people, since forgotten, discovered the elements of science and art, at a time when all other men
were barbarous, and that a race now regarded as the refuse of
society, because their hair is wooly, and their skin is dark, explored
among the phenomena of nature, those civil and religious systems which have since held mankind in awe."[28] De Volney's picture of a black Egypt was derived from the ancient Greek historian

Herodotus, whose influence on Freemasonry has already been noted.[29]

De Volney was not alone in thinking Egypt had been both a black state and the source of Western civilization. In the nineteenth century other French intellectuals such as the Abbé Henri Grégoire also thought that the ancient Egyptians were black and had taught the "venerable and learned men of Greece."[30] As late as 1840 Victor Schoelcher repeated de Volney's claims, "namely, that blacks had founded ancient Egyptian civilization."[31] In nineteenth-century France, the work of de Volney, Grégoire, and Schoelcher was used to defend the idea of black emancipation. But what is also important about this work is that, from its beginnings in the late eighteenth century, it developed into a body of thought among abolitionists that depicted blacks as agents, not objects, of history.

The positive picture accorded black people in the work of these French intellectuals was far from being a universal sentiment, however. Writing at the same time as de Volney, for example, Thomas Jefferson painted a decidedly unflattering portrait of Negroes as both slaves and free people in his *Notes on the State of Virginia*. Although he stated it as a "suspicion," for Jefferson, Negroes were "inferior to...whites in endowments both of body and mind."[32] Most Caucasians in Europe and North America shared his view.[33] This "suspicion" was grounded in a belief that black people had no history.

Long before the emergence of a radical abolitionist movement in North America in 1831, the question of blacks' place in history was a contested issue. In what George Fredrickson has called a "white supremacist" social order, the writing of a history that defended black humanity was deemed important by both black and white abolitionist intellectuals. In nineteenth-century America, Fredrickson has written, "there was a systematic and self-conscious [effort] to make race or color a qualification for membership in the civil community." "Furthermore," he writes, "people of color, however numerous or acculturated they [might] be, [were] treated as permanent aliens or outsiders."[34] The early black historians who celebrated black achievement did not consider themselves either "aliens or outsiders" in the American experience. Their complaint was that history had deliberately excluded them.

Speaking to the American Anti-Slavery Society in 1860, the author and reformer William Wells Brown observed that "history has thrown the colored man out." Brown was not alone in voicing this opinion. The black abolitionist H. Ford Douglass told a Fourth of July audience: "All other races are permitted to travel over the wide field of history and pluck the flowers that bloom there, to glean up heroes, philosophers, sages and poets, and put them into a galaxy of brilliant genius and claim all credit to themselves; but if a black man attempts to do so, he is met at the threshold by the objection, you have no ancestry behind you."[35] Brown and Douglass were responding to the idea, prevalent among most European and American whites during the eighteenth and nineteenth centuries, and as well as the first half of the twentieth century, that blacks were a people without history.

This is not to say that the American Negro was entirely without white champions in the United States. De Volney's claim that the ancient Egyptians were black passed over into the discourse of white American and British abolitionism in the nineteenth century and was also used by black abolitionists. Writing books depicting blacks as people whose past was marked by great accomplishment, Lydia Maria Child, Alexander Hill Everett, Wilson Armistead, and John Stuart Mill described a black past that could have been written either by Herodotus or by de Volney and his peers.[36] "Africa," Child wrote, "was the center, from which religions and scientific light had been diffused. It is well known that Egypt was the great school of knowledge in the ancient world. It was the birth-place of astronomy;...the wisest of the Grecian philosophers, among whom were Solon, Pythagoras and Plato, went there for instruction, as our young men now go to England and Germany."[37] Echoing Child's celebration of a glorious black past, Alexander Hill Everett, a reformer, diplomat, and scholar, after noting that the blacks had not always been degraded, observed:

> It is to Egypt, if to any nation, that we must look as the *real antiqua* mater of the ancient and modern refinement of Europe. The colonies that civilized Greece, the founders of Argos, Athens, Delphi, and so forth came from Egypt, and for centuries afterwards their descendants constantly returned to Egypt as the source and center of civilization.[38]

Everett went on to note: "It appears, in short, that this race, from the deluge down to the conquest of Assyria and Egypt by the Persians, and the fall of Carthage, enjoyed a decided preponderance throughout the whole ancient Western world."[39] Wilson Armistead, a British abolitionist, also defended American blacks by construing them as the progenitors of Western civilization:

> With regard to the intellectual capabilities of the African race, it may be observed that Africa was once the nursery of science and literature, and it was from thence that they were disseminated among the Greeks and Romans. Solon, Plato, Pythagoras, and others of the master spirits of ancient Greece, performed pilgrimages into Africa in search of knowledge; there they set at the feet of ebon philosophers to drink in wisdom.[40]

And the British reformer John Stuart Mill, responding to "The Nigger Question," Thomas Carlyle's racist depiction of West Indian blacks, observed, "The earliest known civilization was, we have reason to believe, a Negro civilization. The original Egyptians are inferred, from the evidence of their sculptures, to have been a Negro race: it was from Negroes, therefore, that the Greeks learnt their first lessons in civilization."[41]

I have quoted Child, Everett, Wilson, and Mill at length because their work, along with the writings of nineteenth-century black thinkers, contested white supremacist claims about the intellectual capability of blacks and their place in history. The idea that blacks were a people without history and were devoid of reason continued to have wide currency both in the general public and scholarly circles through the nineteenth century and into the twentieth. Here, for example, is a taste of George Wilhelm

Friedrich Hegel's thoughts on blacks' place in world history. Writing in 1830–1831, Hegel pronounced that a "want of self-control distinguishes the character of Negroes. This condition is capable of no development or culture, and as we see them at this day, such have they always been."[42] Commenting on the Negroes' "historic barbarism," an article in *Putnam's Monthly* in 1856 reiterated Hegel's claims:

> The most minute and the most careful researches have, as yet, failed to discover a history or any knowledge of ancient times among the negro races. They have invented no writing; not even the rude picture-writing of the lowest tribes. They have no gods and no heroes; no epic poem and no legend, not even simple traditions. There never existed among them an organized government; there never ruled a hierarchy or an established church. Might alone is right. They have never known the arts; they are ignorant even of agriculture. The cities of Africa are vast accumulations of huts and hovels; clay walls or thorny hedges surround them, and pools of blood and rows of skulls adorn their best houses. The few evidences of splendour or civilization are all borrowed from Europe; where there is a religion or creed, it is that of the foreigners; all knowledge, all custom, all progress has come to them from abroad. The negro has no history—he makes no history.[43]

In 1902, Professor John W. Burgess of Columbia University observed, "A black skin means membership in a race of men which has never of itself succeeded in subjecting passion to reason, has never, therefore, created any civilization of any kind."[44] The refusal of many white scholars to see anything positive in the Negroes' past encouraged blacks to write their own history, beginning in the eighteenth and continuing into the twenty-first century.[45]

Carter G. Woodson, the "father of Negro History," noted that white historians made "little effort to set forth what the race has done as a contribution to the world's accumulation of knowledge and the welfare of mankind."[46] The history written by Woodson and his peers came to be called "contributionism" because of its emphasis on Negro contributions to world and American history. Woodson did not invent this mode of historical exposition; what he did was enlarge its database and popularize the study of black history after 1915.[47] "Contributionism" had in fact begun in the eighteenth century, when the Reverends Richard Allen and Absalom Jones published a pamphlet titled *A Narrative of the Proceedings of the Colored People During the Awful Calamity in Philadelphia in the Year 1793, and a Refutation of Some Censures Thrown Upon Them in Some Publications* (1794).[48] The narrative was written to refute charges that Philadelphia's blacks had robbed the sick and had been generally lacking in compassion and civic responsibility during a yellow fever epidemic. The tale told by Allen and Jones detailed the services rendered by black inhabitants of the "City of Brotherly Love" during this crisis. Their history of black contributions during a time of civil disorder is paradigmatic for a number of black newspapers, orations, pamphlets, and histories that were subsequently written in the nineteenth century.

These statements about black historical agency accorded Egypt and Ethiopia a central place in the history of Western civilization. *Freedom's Journal,* America's first black newspaper, which began publishing in 1827, published, according to Bruce Dain, "some dozen long articles and letters or excerpts [concerning] Ancient Africa."[49] Given the fact that this paper was in print for only a year and a half, this was a lot of space to devote to blacks in antiquity. One of the most famous of these articles, entitled "On the Mutability of Human Affairs," appeared in *Freedom's Journal* on April 6, 1827. The anonymous author of this article used the word "mutability" to suggest "the rise and decline of civilizations."[50] If the Egyptians in the nineteenth century, the author writes, were "an ill-looking and slovenly people, immersed in ignorance and sloth," this had not always been the case. On the contrary, "for more than one thousand years [the Egyptians] were the most civilized and enlightened" people on the earth.[51] The message of this essay, placed in a broader context, was that history is not static and that civilizations rise and decline. In other words, white Americans should not assume that their hegemony was infinite.[52]

Ideas about the transitory nature of white supremacy inform both Robert Alexander Young's 1829 protest, *The Ethiopian Manifesto: Issued in Defense of the Black Man's Rights in the Scale of Universal Freedom,* and David Walker's *An Appeal in Four Articles,* also published in 1829.[53] Not much is known about Young. Walker's life, on the other hand, has recently been painstakingly reconstructed by the historian Peter Hinks, whose fascinating book places Walker's pamphlet at the center of a web of pre–Civil War protest and is a marvel of historical detective work.[54]

Of the two documents, David Walker's *Appeal* is more wide-ranging in its condemnation of the treatment of black people in Jacksonian America. The *Appeal* is more than a protest pamphlet —it is also an assertion of the meaning and place of black Americans in history. For Walker, the "Egyptians were Africans or colored people." He goes on to say, "some of them [were] yellow and others dark—a mixture of Ethiopians and the natives of Egypt— about the same as you see the colored people of the United States at the present day."[55] To defend his people against the calumnies of their detractors, Walker gave black people a central role in the creation of Western culture.

> When we take a retrospective view of the arts and sciences— the wise legislators—The Pyramids, and other magnificent buildings—the turning of the channel of the river Nile, by the sons of Africa or of Ham, among whom learning originated, and was carried thence into Greece, where it was improved upon and refined. Thence among the Romans, and all over the then enlightened parts of the world, and it has been enlightening the dark and benighted minds of men from then, down to this day.[56]

Walker's interpretation of history became a central theme of black American history beginning in the 1830s. This can be seen in a number of the histories written to defend the Negroes' claim for equitable treatment in American society. The earliest of these was Robert Benjamin Lewis's 1836 volume *Light and Truth; Collected from the Bible and Ancient and Modern History, Containing the Universal History of the Colored and the Indian Race, From the Creation of the World to the Present Time.* Lewis's book was, in his words, an effort to present "correct knowledge of the colored…people, ancient and modern."[57] Black people are depicted as movers and shakers in Egypt, Ethiopia, Carthage, and Rome. Scipio Africanus, Belisarius, Cicero, Hannibal, Moses, Pompey, Terence, and Tertullian were all black men, according to Lewis.[58]

William Wells Brown added Saint Augustine to this list of black men of achievement in the ancient world.[59] Brown also noted that "the Negro has not always been considered the inferior race. The time was when he stood at the head of science and literature."[60] Brown located the time and place of Negro glory in the ancient world. "It is generally received opinion of the most eminent historians and ethnologists that the Ethiopians were really Negroes."[61] He further contended, "That in the earliest periods of history, the Ethiopians had attained a high degree of civilization…and that to the learning and science derived from them we must ascribe those wonderful monuments which still exist to attest the power and skill of the ancient Egyptians."[62] Thus in Brown's history, Ethiopia, a black country, was the progenitor of Egyptian civilization.

This point of view was shared by the explorer and black nationalist Martin R. Delany and by Presbyterian minister J. W. C. Pennington, who also saw a relationship between Egypt and Ethiopia.[63] According to Delany, "the Negro race comprised the whole native population and ruling people of the upper and lower region of the Nile—Ethiopia and Egypt—excepting those who came by foreign invasion."[64] Frederick Douglass was more cautious than Delany in claiming Egyptian ancestry for the Negro, but after several qualifications, Douglass observed, "While it may not be claimed that the ancient Egyptians were Negroes,—viz.—answering in all respects, to the nations and tribes ranged under the general appellation, Negro; still it may safely be affirmed that a strong affinity and a direct relationship may be claimed by the Negro race, to that grandest of all the nations of antiquity, the builders of the pyramids."[65]

I will return later to the question of whether the ancient Egyptians can accurately be considered black in a racial sense. The important thing to note at this point is that the nineteenth-century black spokesmen who claimed a glorious past for their people did so in order to combat a racist social order. This racism expressed itself not only in the works of white historians such as Hegel and his intellectual heirs but also in the pronouncements of white racist scientists and anthropologists. As Alexander Saxton notes, "Racism became part of that massive synthesis of physical, biological and historical explanation that nineteenth-century science bequeathed to humanity. It then confronted every person, white or non-white, in the dual guise of existing social reality and established scientific knowledge."[66] In the United States of the 1840s and 1850s, this consolidation of racist thought was advanced by the work of the American School of Ethnology, which "affirmed on the basis of new data that the races of mankind had been separately created as distinct and unequal species."[67] According to this group's theory, known as polygenesis, Adam and Eve were not the father and mother of humankind after all, but only of white humanity. Instead of one creation, there were two. The advocates of polygenesis thus posed a challenge to the biblical story of creation and a belief in the unity of humankind set forth in the book of Genesis. Small wonder that blacks responding to this expression of white racism wrote history that affirmed the unity of humankind.[68] Nineteenth-century black historians countering the theory of polygenesis were influenced by the story of the creation and flood in the Bible. To them, God's proclamation in Genesis 11:6, "Behold, the people is one and they have all one language," was more than hyperbole—it was the basis of both their faith and humanity.

While proclaiming the humanity of their people, these historians explained their current low status in terms of a process of degeneration and dispersion. If in these histories ancient Ethiopia and Egypt constituted the apogee of black achievement, the migration of Negroes from these centers of civilization was said to have resulted in their degradation. According to Edward W. Blyden, a West Indian Presbyterian minister, educator, missionary, and racial theorist who lived and worked in nineteenth-century Liberia and Sierra Leone,

> But when in the course of ages, the Ethiopians had wandered into the central and southern regions of Africa, encountering a change of climate and altered character of food and modes of living, they fell into intellectual and physical degradation. This degradation did not consist, however, in change of color....Nor should it be thought strange that the Ethiopians who penetrated into the heart of the African continent should have degenerated, when we consider their distance and isolation from the quickening influence of the arts and sciences in the East.[69]

Ultimately Africa's and the Negroes' "backwardness was explained" in religious terms. African blacks had turned their backs on the one true God. "Polytheism was a grand error," according to Presbyterian minister J. W. C. Pennington.[70] The historian George Washington Williams proclaimed that "the Negro's fall from his high state of civilization" was due to "forgetfulness of God, idolatry."[71] Sin, these men thought, explained the Negroes' plight at the time of European contact with West Africa.

Although these black men argued that their people had a glorious past, they did not think that this heritage—or the subsequent decline from its apogee—was biologically or racially determined. William Wells Brown declared, "There is nothing in race or blood, in color or genetics, that imparts susceptibility of improvement to one race over another."[72] Brown went on to say, "As one man learns from another, so nation learns from nation."[73] In short, "knowledge passed from one people to another."[74] Biological superiority or inferiority was not part of the discourse.

In addition, these early black historians showed no reticence in pointing out to Caucasians that their own history had not always been glorious. "Ancestry [was] something which white Americans should not speak of," William Wells Brown wrote, "unless [their] lips [were in] the dust."[75] The black American Presbyterian minister Henry Highland Garnet also denounced white America. "The besetting sins of the Anglo-Saxon race," Garnet said, "are the love of gain and the love of power."[76] Garnet's denunciation of white America echoed an earlier critique of American racial injustice delivered by David Walker. For Walker, injustice was a constitutive part of white identity, not an aberration, and he traced this attribute historically.

> The whites have always been an unjust, jealous, unmerciful, avaricious and blood thirsty set of beings, always seeking after power and authority—We view them all over the confederacy of Greece, where they were first known to be any thing, [in consequence of education] we see them there, cutting each other's throats—trying to subject each other to wretchedness and misery, to effect which they used all kinds of deceitful, unfair and unmerciful means. We view them next in Rome, where the spirit of tyranny and deceit raged still higher—We view them in Gaul, Spain and in Britain—in fine, we view them all over Europe, together with what were scattered about in Asia and Africa, as heathens, and we see them acting more like devils than accountable men.[77]

Anticipating a question that these characteristics could be applied to any racial group, Walker replied, "But some may ask, did not the blacks of Africa, and the mulattoes of Asia, go on in the same way as did the whites of Europe. I answer no—they never were half so avaricious, deceitful and unmerciful as the whites, according to their knowledge."[78]

Even slavery was not seen as a particular Negro status, as ancient history showed. "But is there anything singular in the fact that in early times Negroes were held in bondage?" asked Blyden. "Was it not the practice among all the early nations to enslave each other?...It was very natural that the more powerful Ethiopians should seize upon the weaker, as is done to this day in certain portions of Africa, and reduce them to slavery."[79]

Ante- and postbellum black historians erected an intellectual edifice that reflected both a belief in progress and a faith in the power of individuals to effect improvements in their own lives and the condition of their race.[80] And while Afrocentrism draws on this tradition of "contributionist" history, it differs from it in conceptualization, argument, and the use of evidence. First, "contributionist" history was for the most part Christian and cosmopolitan. Only Blyden and Delany entertained hopes that black Americans would return to Africa. Second, this record of the black past was not racist but celebratory because it was grounded in a belief in the unity of mankind. Third, "contributionist" history was firmly planted in what Thomas B. Macaulay called the "dross of history," that is, fact. In contrast, Afrocentrism is not a record of the black past, but a therapeutic mythology based on the belief that there is an essential blackness in black people.

What, then, is Afrocentrism and where did it come from in its contemporary form? The idea that blacks have a glorious historical past and a special nature that distinguishes them from whites derives in part from the work of Edward W. Blyden, whose views on the decline of African civilization are quoted above. Called a "pan-Negro patriot" by his biographer Hollis Lynch, Blyden published in the *Methodist Quarterly Review* in 1869 an article entitled "The Negro in Ancient History." This long essay depicted Egypt as a black civilization and challenged the prevailing view in North America and Europe that Negroes had made no contribution to world civilization. Blyden's thinking about race was deeply influenced by two strands of European thought. The first influence was the cosmopolitan nationalism of the German philosopher Johann Gottfried von Herder, whose work in the late eighteenth century "was an important source of nineteenth-century cultural nationalism," according to George Fredrickson.[81] Herder argued that each people had a special spirit or nature, the *Volksgeist*. According to Herder, the *Volksgeist* was the unifying principle of a people's life and culture, the basic strength of a people. Later on in the nineteenth century, Herder's ideas about the *Volksgeist* would be transformed into virulent antiblack racism.[82] Herder himself, however, rejected the idea of racial classification and denied that there was a biological link between people of the same race. For Herder, what bound people together was not biological destiny but cultural and linguistic affinities. Unlike some of his followers, Herder himself was a cosmopolitan who believed in the universal brotherhood of humankind. He did not despise Slavs, Jews, or Negroes, as did a number of his German peers. "A monkey is not your brother," Herder wrote, "but a Negro is, and you should not rob and oppress him."[83]

Edward Blyden used Herder's concept of the *Volksgeist* to create new categories of racial essences, which included what he called the "African Personality."[84] According to Herder, every *Volk* has a "unique contribution," which it alone can make to the progress of humanity as a whole. This cultural contribution is embedded in and exemplified by the *Volk*'s particular language. In Blyden's thought the "African Personality" was Herder's "unique contribution" transvaluated into blackness. The "African Personality," Blyden argued, was the antithesis of the nineteenth-century

European and white American personality. European character, Blyden claimed, was "harsh, individualistic, competitive and combative; European society was highly materialistic: the worship of science and industry replacing God."[85] Africans were the polar opposite of whites because their character embodied "the softer aspects of human nature: cheerfulness, sympathy, willingness to serve, were some of its marked attributes."[86] In Blyden's claim that Africans had a different personality from whites can be seen the genesis of the Afrocentric assertion that contemporary black Americans (called Africans) are "humanitarian rather than individualistic, spiritual and ethical rather than materialistic."[87]

Paradoxically, Blyden's racial theory also drew on the nineteenth century's anti-Negro racialist theorizing. The claim that black people were inferior to whites came from both sides of the Atlantic Ocean. This can be seen in the anti-Negro work of the American Colonization Society, the southern defense of slavery, the English school of anthropology's ethnological claims, and Count Arthur de Gobineau's *Essay on the Inequality of the Races*.[88] Hollis Lynch summarizes the main ideas of these organizations, writings, and individuals in the following manner:

> There was a hierarchy of races with the Negro at or near the bottom; there were "innate and permanent differences in the moral and mental endowments" of races: each race had its "talents," "instincts," and "energy," and that race rather than environmental or circumstantial factors "held the key to the history" of a people; that there existed "an instinctive antipathy among races," and that homogeneity of race was necessary for

successful nation building, that miscegenation was "unnatural," and that mulattoes were "immoral" and weak people with "confused race instincts."[89]

Blyden never accepted the idea of Negro inferiority. Writing about the differences between black and white in 1878, he observed, "There is no absolute or essential superiority on the one side, nor absolute or essential inferiority on the other side." "Each Race," Blyden went on to say, was "equal but distinct"; ultimately, it was a "question of difference of endowment and difference of destiny."[90]

Blyden's theories about race were not completely progressive —hybridity to him meant degeneracy. Because of his experience with the mulatto elites of Liberia and Sierra Leone, Blyden hated mixed-race people. Thus he accepted the theory of "mutual antipathy among races" and the idea that homogeneity of population was essential for the creation of a successful nation state. Blyden once wrote that "no mongrel state can succeed."[91] As I will show later on, Blyden's ideas about the "African Personality," although unacknowledged, reappear in the work of black American Afrocentrists such as Molefi Kete Asante and the Maulana Ronald Karenga.

Another important source of Afrocentrism is the scholarship of the German ethnographer and anthropologist Leo Frobenius. Although Afrocentrists have not acknowledged him as one of their intellectual forefathers, Frobenius's works are central to understanding some of the claims of contemporary Afrocentrism. Frobenius's analysis of pre-Islamic, precolonial African society "was a spirited challenge to the conception of Africa as the 'continent with no history.'"[92] His work was a contestation of the Hegelian stereotype of Africa as a continent without history, which can be seen, for example, in this excerpt from Hegel's *Philosophy of History*: "At this point we leave Africa, not to mention it again. For it is no historical part of the world, it has no movement or development to exhibit. Historical movement in it—that is in its northern part—belongs to the Asiatic or European world."[93] Frobenius's work had a profound impact on a number of black francophone intellectuals such as Aíme Cesaire; Cheikh Anta Diop, founder of the historical school of Négritude; and Léopold Sénghor, late president of Senegal and one of the fathers of the mythopoetic branch of Négritude. Sénghor has written that Frobenius's books were "sacred" to his generation. "He spoke to us," Sénghor says, "of the only problem which preoccupied us: the nature, value, and destiny of Black African culture."[94]

Frobenius's work was a "catalyst" that encouraged Sénghor and Diop to see that Africa had both culture and history.[95] It satisfied a deep psychological need in these black African intellectuals, who lived in a world that said their people had no history. "The idea of the barbarous Negro," Frobenius declared, "is a European invention."[96] Frobenius's scholarship on Africa, first published in the 1890s, was a radical departure from his early anthropological work.[97] Prior to this, anthropology had been concerned with the collection and description of ethnographic facts. Frobenius suggested a "structure for organizing those facts." Employing a theory that combined culture and history, he created a methodology that unified the work of anthropologists and historians, and enabled him to focus on the origins of culture.[98] His ethnographies were comparative and examined widely scattered cultures with the intent of tracing them back to common origins.[99]

Writing in the tradition of Herder, Frobenius created his own categories of the *Volksgeist* for West Africa, dividing the region into two cultural areas with differing worldviews, or attitudes toward life. As frames of reference, these two worldviews, which he labeled Hamitic and Ethiopian, were not dichotomized; that is, they were not absolute but relative.[100] Furthermore, this schema "had nothing to do with race or color, but was purely a cultural classification," says J .M. Ita.[101] For within the West African context, Ita continues, "both groups are equally black."[102] What was the practical meaning of Frobenius's theory?

The societies Frobenius called Ethiopian were those of black Africans living in social organizations that were acephalous, or stateless. The Mandingos and Hausas of West Africa, by contrast, were not Ethiopians but Hamites, he claimed, because they "had well-developed states."[103] Hamitism, according to Frobenius, was characterized by "magic, the attempt to dominate nature by mechanical means such as spells, incantations, or scientific devices." Ethiopians were the exact opposite of Hamites. Ethiopianism was mystical, "being in union with nature and therefore not trying to dominate her from outside."[104]

Frobenius's conception of "Hamitic" and "Ethiopian" was based not on empirical research in Africa but on what the German anthropologist thought about France.[105] Frobenius considered France and England Hamitic civilizations—cultures driven by reason and instrumentalism. Germans and Russians, on the other hand, "were an 'inward' or 'spiritual' people."[106] The German state was organic; it was an "'organism'…based on the natural unit of the extended family or clan" and had evolved over time.[107] In the context of nineteenth-century politics, the "organic state" was a conservative ideal. Both German and Russian nationalists during this time argued that autocratic or authoritarian regimes were best for their people.

This claim was a reaction against the cosmopolitanism and materialism of France before and after the French Revolution. In Germany, Isaiah Berlin observes, the reaction to France "politically, culturally, militarily" was extreme.[108] Berlin describes the German reaction to France in this way:

> The humiliated and defeated Germans, particularly the traditional, religious, economically backward East Prussians, bullied by French officials imported by Frederick the Great, responded, like the bent twig of the poet Schiller's theory, by lashing back and refusing to accept their alleged inferiority. They discovered in themselves qualities far superior to those of their tormentors. They contrasted their own deep, inner life of the spirit, their own profound humility, their selfless pursuit of true values—simple, noble, sublime—with the rich, worldly, successful, superficial, smooth, heatless, morally empty French. This mood rose to fever pitch during the national resistance to Napoleon, and was indeed the original exemplar of the reaction of many a backward, exploited, or at any rate patronised society, which, resentful of the apparent inferiority of its status, reacted by turning to real or imaginary

triumphs and glories in its past, or enviable attributes of its own national or cultural character.[109]

Berlin concludes this observation by stating that "those who cannot boast of great political, military or economic achievements, or a magnificent tradition of art or thought, seek comfort and strength in the notion of the free and creative life of the spirit within them, uncorrupted by the vices of power or sophistication."[110] If Frobenius saw France as the epitome of the corruption that characterized Western life, in West Africa he found an antidote to Western civilization. He was fascinated by what he called "the childhood of man."[111] West Africa, to him, was a place of primitive spontaneity, where man lived in touch with himself and his roots in nature.

In his criticism of the West, Frobenius attracted the attention of a number of West African students in Paris, including Diop and Sénghor. Both Diop and Sénghor, central players in the development of the Négritude movement that was the intellectual forerunner of Afrocentrism, found in Frobenius's work a means to defend their indigenous cultures. Frobenius's universal historical scheme, for example, enabled Sénghor to fit the Hamitic/Ethiopian opposition into a paradigm that assigned a place to black African civilization in "la civilization humaine."[112] Like the later Afrocentrists, the proponents of Négritude were resentful of their status as cultural and historical objects. This frame of mind expresses itself in what Nietzsche called *ressentiment*. As Liah Greenfeld has recently written, "The creative power of *ressentiment*—and its sociological importance—consists in that it may eventually lead to the 'transvaluation of values,' that is, to the transformation of the value scale in a way which denigrates the originally supreme values, replacing them with notions which are unimportant, external, or indeed bear in the original scale the negative sign."[113] Greenfeld goes on to note that the term "transvaluation of values" may be "somewhat misleading" because the process of appropriation "is not a direct reversal of the original hierarchy." "*Ressentiment* is by definition a reaction to the values of others," Greenfeld says, "and not to one's own condition regardless of others, the new system of values that emerges is necessarily influenced by the one to which it is a reaction."[114] What is important here is the word "reaction" because Blyden's concept of the "African Personality," Négritude, and ultimately Afrocentrism is all reaction to the West that, although challenging European (or "white") values, nevertheless frames their arguments in terms of Western (or European or "white") values and terminology. Afrocentrism does this when it claims that blacks were the originators of Western civilization. I would add that the responses of black American intellectuals to both the West and Africa have fluctuated with the varying conditions of race relations in the United States.

In the 1850s, for example, Martin R. Delany was a leading proponent of emigration—a voluntary movement of black people out of the United States to West Africa.[115] Emigration was the black response to the program of the American Colonization Society, which wanted to resettle American free Negroes in its colony of Liberia. Delany was a savage critic of both the society and its West African colony. Liberia, according to Delany, was problematic as a nation. "Liberia is not an Independent Republic: in fact," Delany said, "it is not an independent nation at all; but a poor miserable mockery—a burlesque on a government—a pitiful dependency on the American colonizationist."[116] Delany wanted black Americans to establish an independent black nation in Africa, free of white control. This black state would serve as a protector of Negro people throughout the world. In this capacity, Delany's nation would raise cotton, which could be sold on the international market and thus reduce the high profits being earned by American slave owners. Delany thought that a worldwide depression in cotton prices would force the American planters to emancipate their slaves.[117]

Underlying and accompanying this grandiose scheme of racial uplift were some mainstream Western attitudes about Africa. Delany and other emigrationists wanted to create a black Protestant nation in West Africa to "elevate" and "Christianize" the natives.[118] Delany and his black peers were not cultural relativists. Like most educated people of the Victorian era, these black Americans believed that there was only one culture. All other cultures and religions, they thought, represented a deviation from the high standards established by Protestant Christianity. The Reverend Alexander Crummell, a black Episcopal missionary in West Africa, had the following things to say about Africa:

> Africa lies low and is wretched. She is the maimed and crippled arm of humanity. Her great powers are wasted. Dislocation and anguish have reached every joint. Her condition in every point calls for succor—moral, social, domestic, political, commercial, and intellectual.…Africa is the victim of her het-

erogeneous idolatries. Africa is wasting away beneath the accretions of civil and moral miseries. Darkness covers the land, and gross darkness covers the people. Great social evils universally prevail. Confidence and security are destroyed. Licentiousness abounds everywhere. Moloch rules and reigns throughout the whole continent, and by the ordeal of Sassy-wood, Fetishes, human sacrifices, and devil-worship, is devouring men, women, and little children. They have not the Gospel. They are living without God. The Cross has never met their gaze, and its consolations have never entered their hearts, nor its everlasting truths cheered their deaths.[119]

Neither Crummell nor Delany was interested in returning to Africa to "get down" with the natives. In this, nineteenth-century black nationalism stands in sharp contrast to modern black cultural nationalism, which celebrates Africa as a site of racial and cultural authenticity in reaction to the racial problems of black people in the United States today. Such cultural nationalism is also a rejection of Western culture as soulless and machinelike. In short, modern cultural black nationalism has rejected the West on both cultural and political grounds as inappropriate for what Blyden called the "African Personality." When read in this context, Afrocentrism is a black American version of Négritude, and both are textbook examples of *ressentiment* and the "transvaluation of values."

As propounded by Sénghor in the 1930s, Négritude was a form of what the French anthropologist called "primitive mentality." For Sénghor the idea of the primitive did not connote inferiority or a lack of sophistication.[120] It was, however, a site of rebellion against European colonization. "We were in revolt against order, against the values of the West, and especially against Reason," Sénghor has said. "We opposed to the platitudes of reason the lofty tree tops of our forest."[121] What does this elegant denunciation of the West mean? The West African scholar Abiola Irele unpacks Sénghor's quip with great insight when he comments, "For Sénghor, each people, race, and civilization has its own manner of envisaging the world, and each manner is as valid ultimately as another. The African manner is rooted in the values of emotion rather than in the logical categories historically developed in the tradition of European rationalism, and it is as valid in its own terms as the European, hence his well-known dictum: Emotion is African as Reason is Hellenic."[122] Within francophone Africa, the popularity of Négritude may be explained because it provided a coherent concept of identity, which gave the colonized blacks "a sense of the Africans' separate cultural and spiritual inheritance."[123] This sensibility was enhanced by the work of Cheikh Anta Diop, the Senégalese humanist, scientist, and political rival of Sénghor.

Diop and Sénghor were both nationalists, but their opposition to French colonialism was expressed differently. Sénghor's nationalism was mystical and poetic, whereas Diop's occupied another analytical space. These points of view can be read as either complementary or antithetical. What specifically distinguished Diop's from Sénghor's was its emphasis on the concrete. In an interview published in 1989 Diop described his work in the following terms: "my work in history, sociology and linguistics kept to the path of objective verifiable reality. By throwing light on the falsifications to which the historical past of the black man has been subjected, these historical, sociological and linguistic studies serve to reinforce the cultural personality of the Africans."[124]

Diop's work, which he called "historical sociology," challenged the European imperialist argument that black Africans had no culture or history. This can be seen in his first book, *Nations, Negres, et Culture*, translated into English as *The African Origin of Civilization*.[125] Diop's work was interdisciplinary, involving the use of both the natural sciences and the humanities. His primary objective was to demonstrate the Negro origins of ancient Egyptian civilization and establish continuities between pharaonic Egypt and the African cultures of the 1940s and 1950s.[126] To do this, Diop repeated the arguments of Blyden and the eighteenth- and nineteenth-century abolitionists about the genealogy of Western culture.[127] Concerned with establishing a historically grounded identity for Africans, Diop proclaimed, "We must restore the historical consciousness of the African peoples and reconquer a Promethean consciousness."[128] Psychic liberation from the intellectual hegemony of Western thought was a prerequisite for black liberation, Diop maintained. "Consequently, the Black man must become able to restore the continuity of his national historic past, to draw from it the moral advantage needed to reconquer his place in the modern world, without falling into the excess of a Nazism in reverse."[129]

Although both Sénghor's and Diop's Négritude drew on the romantic racialism of the eighteenth and nineteenth centuries, it was not racist, since both of these West African intellectuals were bicultural, that is, African and French (to the extent that they were educated in the French *metropole*). And while the work of Sénghor and Diop could be labeled racist by some because of its emphasis on transhistoric "essences" in black Africans, these qualities were construed as being cultural, not biological. Because Négritude was a reaction to a racial essentialism that proclaimed that black Africans were without either culture or history, it was, then, a contestation of colonialist ideology. This cannot be said of the contemporary Afrocentric movement in the United States.

Some of the claims about black people's place in antiquity that we associate today with Afrocentrism can be found in the following older works: W. L. Hunter, *Jesus Christ Had Negro Blood in His Veins* (1901); Joseph H. Haynes, *The Amonian or Hamitic Origins of the Ancient Greeks, Cretans, and All of the Celtic Races* (1905); William F. Ferris, *The African Abroad* (1913, 2 vols.); W. E. B. Du Bois, *The Negro* ([1915] 1970); George W. Parker, *The Children of the Sun* ([1918] 1978); Carter G. Woodson and Charles Wesley, *The Negro in Our History* ([1922] 1978); W. E. B. Du Bois, *Black Folk Then and Now* ([1939] 1978); J. A. Rogers, *World's Great Men of Color* ([1946] 1972, 2 vols.); and John Hope Franklin, *From Slavery to Freedom* (1963). Although he was not an Afrocentrist, Marcus Garvey also expressed ideas from time to time that today would be considered Afrocentric: "When the white race of today had no civilization of its own, when white men lived in caves and were counted as savages, this race of ours boasted of a wonderful civilization on the banks of the Nile."[130] Garvey also urged blacks to develop their own "thoughts" (ideas). He told his followers that a race that failed to think independently would remain slaves.[131]

Garvey called this process of thought "African Fundamentalism." Its goal was the emancipation of "the Negro from the thoughts of others."[132] The emphasis in Garvey's work on changing the way black people think occupies a central place in contemporary Afrocentric discourse. Claims about the need to reorient black thinking and Egypt may also be found in the autobiography and speeches of Malcolm X.[133] Finally, the late St. Clair Drake published in 1987 a wide-ranging study of blacks and Africa in the ancient world.[134]

According to Stephen Howe, Afrocentrism as an academic school developed out of a split in the predominantly white African Studies Association (ASA) in 1968, when the late John H. Clarke formed a black caucus within the ASA. From these activities came the all-black African Heritage Studies Association (AHSA). The aims of the AHSA, Clarke proclaimed, were "reconstruction of African History and cultural studies along Afrocentric lines while effecting an intellectual union among black scholars the world over."[135] As it is used today, the term "Afrocentrism" has no one meaning, nor is it solely concerned with the study of history. Afrocentric scholars work in a variety of disciplines, including biology, education, history, and psychology.[136] But central to all of these areas of inquiry is a particular conception of the past. Within this historical discourse there are some dubious assumptions. First, there is the idea that there is a unified African culture that transcends time and space. Second, there is a faulty rhetorical framework that privileges the synchronic over the diachronic. Third, there is a delusion that one can be re-embedded in a past that never existed. And overall, there is a paucity of empirical evidence to support these assumptions. I would like to illustrate these four points by taking a look at the work of Molefi Kete Asante and other Afrocentric scholars writing in the United States today.

Although Afrocentrism is a loose term that applies to a number of disciplines, Asante and his peers' brand of Egyptian-centered Afrocentric history is the most widely espoused version of it in contemporary America. According to Asante, Afrocentrism places "African ideas and values at the center of inquiry."[137] What Asante means by this is not clear. Furthermore, "centering" oneself in an ideology may result in either ethnocentrism or solipsism. In the case of Afrocentrism, just what set of African values is Asante asking black Americans to center themselves in? Ashanti, Congo, Hausa, Hutu, Ibo, Zulu—these African tribal names indicate that the peoples of Africa have no unified culture or set of values. As the recent internecine wars in Angola, Liberia, Rwanda, Sudan, and Zaire suggest, the only thing some Africans have in common is the color of their skin, and this is not a tie that binds or overrides particularity. Even the movement for political independence, as the recent black struggles in South Africa have shown, was not enough to unite the Cape Coloureds with the rest of the black population. A number of the Cape Coloureds voted for the white regime and thus opposed the candidates of the African National Congress. The Xhosa, a black tribal group in South Africa, expressed their contempt for the Coloureds by saying, "You people have nothing—no language of your own, no culture. You are remnants."[138]

Writing about the problem of black cultural unity, K. Anthony Appiah has noted, "We do not have a common traditional culture, common language, a common religious or conceptual vocabulary....We do not even belong to a common race."[139] Edward Blyden made this point with telling force when he wrote:

> There are Negroes and Negroes. The numerous tribes inhabiting the vast continent of Africa can no more be regarded as in every respect equal than the numerous peoples of Asia or Europe can be so regarded. There are the same tribal or family varieties inhabiting the region of the upper Niger, the Mandingoes, the Hausas, the Bornous of Senegambia, the Nubas of the Nile region, or Dafoor and Kordofan, the Ashantees, Fantees, Dahomians, Yorubas, and that whole class of tribes occupying the eastern and middle and western portions of the continent north of the equator. Then there are the tribes of lower Guinea and Angola....and in speaking of them they are frequently characterized in one or two sentences. Now it should be evident that no short description can include all these people; no single definition, however comprehensive, can embrace them all.[140]

These two quotations indicate the impossibility of subsuming a complex multicultural site such as Africa under a unitary rubric such as Afrocentrism.

Even if I were to concede the possibility of black Americans' reappropriating or getting in touch with what Henry Louis Gates Jr. has called their "inner African," as Asante urges us to, the method Asante suggests for accomplishing this goal is questionable.[141] According to Asante, Afrocentrism or Africalogy is defined...as the Afrocentric study of phenomena, events, ideas, and personalities related to Africa. The mere study of phenomena of Africa is not Africalogy but some other intellectual enterprise. The scholar who generates research questions based on the centrality of Africa is engaged in a very different research inquiry than the one who imposes Western criteria on the phenomena.

As Asante almost incomprehensibly adds:

The uses of African origins of civilization and the Kemetic high culture as a classical starting point are the practical manifestations of the ways the scholar secures centrism when studying Africa. Africalogy uses the classical starting place as the beginning of knowledge. This is why Afrocentric is perhaps the most important word in the above definition of Africalogy. Otherwise one could easily think that any study of African phenomena or people constitutes Africalogy.[142]

Asante's definition of Africalogy, to paraphrase Paul Gilroy, is "an invariant, anti-historical [or ahistorical] notion of black particularity to which [Asante and his followers] alone...maintain privileged access."[143] This is because Africalogy is a totalizing therapeutic mythology without internal discourse or the potential of discourse with other scholarship. One either accepts its problematic fundamental premise about "the African origins of civilization" or rejects it. It is one thing, for example, to say that anthropology has established the fact that "life" began in Africa in humanoid form.

It is another thing to extrapolate from this fact that "civilization" began in Africa. The conflation of these two words, "life" and "civilization," is a clever strategy, but not a very useful one for the study of the past. It ignores the possibility that civilization could have and did have multiple origins in places other than Africa and, specifically, the Nile River Valley.

In focusing on ancient Egypt as a site of black achievement, Afrocentrists like Asante create an idealized mythic space that stands in opposition to the present grim reality of black inner-city America. This is exemplary of the faulty synchronic thinking that pervades Afrocentrism. Egypt was a patrimonial state in which everything was owned by the pharaoh. The land held by the nobles, officials, priests, temples, or private citizens was an expression of the god-king's beneficence. The pharaohs could always take back the property they granted to the state's elite, but this was seldom done.[144] In the name of the pharaoh, the Egyptian state was administered by a bureaucracy ensuring that the kingdom's material resources were allocated in a way that maintained social stability. The principal task of this officialdom was to manage the "economic environment for the benefit of the elite," and when this was well done, "benefit was incidentally spread to a significant sector of the population."[145]

Peasant farmers constituted the largest section of the Egyptian population. In ancient Egypt, peasants were excused from military service because they worked the land. When they were not working in agriculture, these peasants performed corvée labor, building the huge pyramids that served as the pharaohs' tombs. Egyptian common people also labored in the country's quarries and mines, strengthened dikes, and cleared and deepened canals.[146] Conscription of peasant labor enabled the Egyptian bureaucracy to acquire a larger labor force than would normally have been available if the officials had needed to rely solely on those people who worked either part-time or full-time for the state. The peasants who labored on these official projects had some recompense for their labor in the form of rations. Even so, tasks the workers were ordered to perform were arduous, and some of the corvée laborers resisted their state service. This can be seen in an official document taken from the late middle kingdom, a prison register, which reveals how a woman who chose not to perform her duties was treated:

> The daughter of Sa-anhur, Teti, under the Scribe of the Fields of the city of This: a woman. An order was issued to the Great Prison in year 31, 3rd month of summer, day 9, to release her family from the courts, and at the same time to execute against her the law pertaining to one who runs away without performing his service. Present [check mark]. Statement by the Scribe of the Vizier, Deduamun: "Carried out; case closed."[147]

Evidence such as this, fragmentary though it may be, clearly indicates the authoritarian nature of the pharaoh's regime. In their glorification of Egypt as a black civilization, the Afrocentrists have ignored the coercive power of the god-king's state and its intrusion into the lives of the common people.

This point and several others are missed in Asante's discussion of what he calls the "Egyptian caste system."[148] For example,

Asante writes that "Egyptian society was based on a caste system. You were born into your caste, or social position and role."[149] However, this conceptualization of social relations in ancient Egypt is incorrect. Egyptian society was hierarchical but not caste based like that of Hindu India, whose caste system is based on religious ideas of blood purity and impurity. Members of the different Hindu castes have traditionally been forbidden to intermarry or associate with each other to avoid ritual and blood pollution. Hindu society to this day continues to be endogamous, unlike pharaonic Egypt, where the only social custom similar to endogamy was the pharaoh's marriage to his sister.[150]

Asante's misunderstanding of the social structure of Egyptian society creates even more confusion when he describes the "laborers and soldiers" of ancient Egypt as a "middle caste of people with everyday jobs" and then in the next sentence asserts that "they were like the middle class in the United States."[151] The terms "middle caste" and "middle class" cannot be conflated, since they connote different social statuses and do not occupy the same analytical space. Furthermore, the word "class" has economic, political, and cultural meanings that Asante's imprecise usage does not comprehend. Asante tries to resolve this problem by noting that there was some flexibility in the Egyptian social hierarchy: "the Pharaoh could change a person's status by bestowing special favor."[152] However, his emphasis on the flexible nature of ancient Egyptian society is best understood as an avoidance of the issue of class conflict in antiquity and Africa in general.

Given that Asante calls himself a "Diopian," this is strange, in view of the fact that Diop himself was very much concerned with the issue of class and social conflict in Egypt and black Africa. Diop assigned the beginning of this conflict to the Sixth Dynasty of the Old Kingdom of Egypt, which "was to end with the first popular uprising in Egyptian history."[153] Pitting rich against poor, the rebellion tore the realm apart, according to Diop. "The wretched of Memphis...pillaged the city, robbing the rich and driving them into the streets."[154] Pharaonic Egypt's hierarchically determined social mobility was radically different from the process whereby social status is acquired in the modern world. What Asante has done both here and in his muddled explanation of Egyptian castes is characteristic of the historical writing of Afrocentrists in general. Afrocentrism flattens out the past and fails to contextualize ideas, giving it a presentist framework rather than a historical one. This can be seen most glaringly if we return to Afrocentrism's use of "race" or biology in the ancient world to invent a past that never was.

The people of ancient Egypt were of mixed genetic background. Their roots lay not only in Africa but also in the Mediterranean and Asia Minor.[155] The ancient Egyptians did not think of people in terms of black or white races. "The whole matter of black or white Egyptians is a chimera," Frank Yurco writes, "cultural baggage from our own society that can only be imposed artificially on ancient Egyptian society."[156] Continuing, Yurco informs us that "the ancient Egyptians, like their modern descendants, were of varying complexions of color, from the light Mediterranean type (like Nefertiti) to the light brown of Middle Egypt to the darker brown of upper Egypt, to the darkest shade around Aswan and the First Cataract region, where even today, the population shifts to Nubian."[157] Because the Egyptians were not race conscious in a modern sense, they conscripted enemies into their own army and allowed these people to be absorbed into Nile Valley society, even though they came from different ethnic backgrounds. The integration of various types of people into the Egyptian military created a state whose population was heterogeneous. At various moments in ancient history, Nubians and Semites serving in the pharaoh's war machine were given land as bonuses on retirement, intermarried with the Egyptians, and produced a mixed progeny.[158]

The fact that the Egyptians married the people they subjugated does not mean they thought of them as equals, however. This can be seen in their attitudes toward the Nubians. Nubia, or Kush, as it was called in the ancient world, is the modern-day Sudan. The Egyptians called Nubia "miserable Kush" and thought the country and its people were backward.[159] For the Egyptians, Nubia was a source of raw materials and slaves. When Pharaoh Thutmose I conquered Nubia, his scribes wrote this of the "Lord of the Two Lands":

> He hath overthrown the chief of the [Nubians]; the Negro is [helpless, defenseless] in his grasp. He hath united the boundaries of this two sides, there is not a remnant among the Curly-Haired, who come to attack him; there is not a single survivor among them. The Nubian Troglodytes fall by the sword, and are thrust aside in their lands; their foulness, it floods their valleys; the [ ] of their mouths is like a violent flood. The fragments cut from them are too much for the birds, carrying off the prey to another place.[160]

On another occasion, the chronicler wrote that Thutmose "sailed down-river, with all countries in his grasp, that wretched Nubian Troglodyte being hanged head downward at the [prow] of the ba[rge] of his majesty, and landed at Karnak."[161] The Nubians were only one of the many peoples expansionist Egypt brought under its sway. Egyptian overlordship in Nubia lasted for more than 2,000 years, and this relationship can be traced from the earliest beginnings of Egypt down until its demise.[162] Nubia also conquered Egypt and ruled there from 747 to 656 B.C. To legitimate themselves as rulers of Upper and Lower Egypt, the Nubian pharaohs adopted the styles and titles of their former overlords,[163] just as the Mongol and Manchu emperors of China enhanced their authority by adopting the title "Son of Heaven." Like imperial China, ancient Egypt was a civilization that conquered, was conquered, and conquered its conquerors. Afrocentrism's simplistic, racializing approach to the study of history is woefully inadequate, given the complexities of conquest, subjugation, cultural diffusion, and cultural appropriation in the ancient world.

In their effort to create a usable and glorious past for today's black Americans, the Afrocentrists have read modern racial categories back into a world where they had no meaning. Slavery, for example, was not racial in the ancient world, as it was in the Americas. Among the ancients, slavery cut across racial and class lines. The nineteenth-century historian George Washington Williams understood this when he wrote of ancient slavery that it "was not, at this time, confined to any particular race."[164] Williams's observation indicates that race cannot be read as a transhistorical category in the study of the past. To understand the ancient world, we have to abandon race as a marker of social status. It has no meaning in this context, since race is a problematic construct when projected into a realm in which social status had other bases. Since race is a social construct, not a biological datum as the Afrocentrists claim, we have to be skeptical of their reading of Egypt as a black civilization.

In defining race as a social construct, I do not want to suggest that it is unreal. As a lived category, race has both material and discursive consequences for people defined as racial subjects, but as I am using it here it is nonessentialist and nonbiological. I understand race to be an ascriptive category that is historically, socially, and politically determined and that shifts over time.[165] In Afrocentrist literature, this process is elided to claim Egypt as a site of origin for Western civilization; this gives Afrocentrist history a biological subtext. Because, in the Afrocentrists' view, Egypt was a black country whose cultural production was copied by Greece and Rome, what we call "Western civilization" derives from Africa, the place of "source and origin."[166] In short, the "brothers and sisters" have out-Greeked the Greeks.

The question that must be asked at this point is, Were the Ethiopians and Egyptians Negroes? The answer to this query is not straightforward. When, for example, in 1903 the Ethiopian emperor Menilek II was asked "to become honorary president of the Society for the Uplift of Negroes," His Imperial Majesty responded, "Yours is an excellent idea; the Negro should be uplifted, but I am not a Negro."[167] Historically the Ethiopian upper class did not consider itself negroid. Indeed, these people used a derogatory term, "Shangalla" or "Shankalla," to describe people whose skin was darker than theirs. The word "Shankalla," one authority has written, "referred to a whole range of peripheral peoples with overtones of the American English 'nigger.'"[168] In the ancient world there were no "Negroes" or "Niggers"; thus the people whom the Greeks called Ethiopian were not Negroes as we use the term today. The concept of race as currently employed "was unknown to the ancient Egyptians. Non-Egyptians were identified by their ethnic tribal affiliations or by the region/country from which they came."[169] In short, color did not operate in this context the way it does in contemporary America.

According to classicist Frank Snowden, "Frequent references to color indicate that the word Ethiopian designated persons of varying degrees of blackness. Furthermore, the association of various combinations of other physical characteristics with the Ethiopians suggests that the Greeks and Romans were describing two types of people whom anthropologists today would classify as subtypes of the Negroid race."[170] And writing eighty-seven years before Snowden, George Washington Williams, the author of America's most thoroughly researched nineteenth-century history of black Americans, observed:

> But while it is a fact, supported by both sacred and profane history, that the terms "cush" and "Ethiopian" were used interchangeably, there seems to be no lack of proof that the same terms were applied frequently to a people who were not Negroes. It should be remembered, moreover, that there were nations who were black and yet not Negroes.[171]

Snowden and Williams support the idea that race is a socially defined category and not a biological datum. The fact that some nineteenth-century blacks called the people of Ethiopia and Egypt "black" does not mean that these people thought of themselves as black or were even perceived by their peers as being black. What this suggests is that in classical texts the word "Ethiopian" refers to color, not race. The word "black" does not have a transhistoric meaning, as the Afrocentrists would have us think.

Color is no indication of race. The Roman playwright Petronius understood this problem when he had one of the characters in the *Satyricon* suggest as a practical joke that he and some of his friends dye their "hair, nails, everything" to become black. The suggestion is shown to be of limited utility by his additional comment: "As if this colour alone could alter our shapes, and it were not needed that many things act in unison to make a good lie on all accounts. Suppose the stain of dye on the face could last for some time; imagine that never a drop of water could make any mark in our skins, nor our clothes stick to the ink."[172] This observation is followed in turn by a comment that should be noted by anyone attempting to read contemporary racial categories into the ancient world: "Artificial colours dirty one's body without altering it."

To the Romans of Petronius' day, to be a black African had a specific meaning. "In a discussion of blacks," according to the classicist Lloyd Thompson, "in the Roman world (as distinct from the remote African habitats often assigned to the so-called Aethiopes by geographers, ethnographers and mythographers), the relevant concept is clearly that of an anthropological type distinctly black in colour (according to Roman perceptions)."[173]

What were Roman perceptions of African blacks? The people whom the Romans designated Aethiopes (blacks) were a distinct somatic type. These people had a "distinct physiognomy constituted not only by skin-colour, but by a combination of traits which at least resembled the stereotype of black skin, crinkly hair, thick lips, and flat nose described by Petronius and other writers."[174] In the Roman perception of blackness, color was the most distinguishing signifier. The other physical attributes "broad or flat noses (or 'snub noses'), thickness of lip, and hair types meriting the descriptions 'wooly' or 'curly' or 'tightly-curled' were not peculiar to the Aethiopes." Curly or tightly-curled hair was also characteristic of both the Moors and the Egyptians the Romans encountered. Greeks and Nordics had snub noses and people who were nonblack were known to have both dark skin and thick lips in the Roman world.[175] As the Roman example indicates, what is called black is a function of time, place, power, and perception.[176]

The assertion that ancient Egypt was a black society derives in part from a selective reading of Egyptian cultural production as biological. This is not a very fruitful or insightful way to understand either race or the past, as one scholar has written. "The literature dealing with the racial history of Egypt [and Nubia] provides an outstanding example of the danger of assessing biological relationships from cultural evidence."[177] The cultural evidence employed by Afrocentrists to show that ancient Egypt was a black society consists of three types: monuments, paintings, and mummies. But these artifacts have to be read with a subtlety lacking in Afrocentrist analysis.[178] The racialized Afrocentric interpretation of Egyptian art is a product of present racial problems that "have been imposed on the material remains of a past culture even though these remains do not in themselves denote race."[179]

An examination of the social function of Egyptian art reveals the shortcomings of racialized readings. The styles of Egyptian art were established in the First Dynasty (ca. 3050 B.C.). This representation of form, according to the archaeologist Kathryn A. Bard, did not represent humans "as seen in perspective by the eye." The pictures depict their subjects in a fashion that "transforms reality. The head, arms, and legs are drawn in profile, the torso is depicted frontally." Bard continues with an observation clear to anyone familiar with authoritarian art: "The conventions of Egyptian art were those of the crown, and what is characteristic of Egyptian style in art for the most part represents a very small segment of the population."[180] Egyptian art expressed the hegemonic pretensions of an elite and cannot be taken as a depiction of reality. Thus when Asante asserts that "the ancient paintings give us a picture of Egypt as seen through ancient Egyptian eyes," he errs.[181] Writing in 1857, Edward Blyden noted the limitations of reading Egyptian monuments as a sign of racial designation: "The monuments are neither intended to furnish, nor can they furnish a complete delineation of all branches of public and private life, of all the products and phenomena of the whole, animal, vegetable, and mineral creation of the country. They cannot be viewed as a complete cyclopedia of Egyptian customs and civilization."[182] Egyptian art was highly stylized and based on references that were mythic and idealized. This process can be seen most clearly in pictures of the pharaoh and royal family, where pageant, ritual, myth, and insignia established the divinity of the god-king and his relatives. Accompanied by worshipful language, these pictures constituted a record of Egyptian rulers' accomplishments from coronation to death. When placed in the context through which royalty claims to be different from ordinary humans, this art had more than an aesthetic or a racial purpose. In Egyptian as in other royalist systems, the numerous monuments, temples, tombs, obelisks, and so on, which were erected to honor rulers living and dead, served to establish the authority of the ruler by linking the sovereign to the past and present history of the Egyptian state.[183]

Even when the Egyptians drew themselves, they depicted the coloration of men and women differently. This art was gendered, with men portrayed as having black or dark complexions and women in lighter tones, which does not warrant concluding that in general Egyptian men were darker than Egyptian women. It should be noted that this was only one of several forms of painting produced by the Egyptians and therefore cannot be used as an indicator of that society's racial composition.[184] When Egyptian art focused on subject peoples such as non-Egyptian Africans or Asiatics, these people were painted as different from their conquerors.[185] Subject peoples are portrayed, by means of their clothing and hairstyles, as "others." The Nubians who brought tribute to the court of Thutmose II, for example, were painted in darker colors than the Asiatics. The Nubians also have more prognathous jaws, a physical feature that differentiated them from Egyptians. Despite the efforts of the Afrocentrist to make prognathism a physical trait of Nubians, it is not. A visitor to the Hapsburg royal palace in Vienna will see from the family's portraits that prognathous jaws were common in that European royal family and are thus not solely a negroid trait. Egyptians also drew the Nubians with neck markings and scarification, two forms of adornment that the Egyptians did not practice. Even the hairstyles and earrings worn by the Nubians were different from those of the Egyptians. This process of distinguishing difference cut across gender and ethnic lines and showed how Nubian women differed from their Egyptian counterparts. In one panel of a picture showing subject peoples presenting tribute to Thutmose III, an elite Nubian woman is shown standing in an ox-drawn cart. Egyptian women would never have been painted this way because they did not ride in ox carts. Race is not important in these pictures; what is emphasized is ethnicity.[186]

Nor can the race of the Egyptians be determined by examining their mummies, at least not as Cheikh Anta Diop tried to do it. Indeed, Diop's work represents probably the single most unsuccessful effort on the part of a scholar to determine the racial origins of an Egyptian notable. In an essay on Pharaoh Ramses II, Diop tells his readers that he was able to determine Ramses's race by looking at "Egyptian mummies at the Paris Musée de l'Homme." Diop states without qualification that "Ramses II was black," adding that "science, by isolating the Sutter and Gm6 factors and analyzing the percentage of melanin can determine precisely the race of Ramses II through the most objective of methods."[187] These methods may be accurate and objective, but they tell us nothing if they are distorted by the ideology of racial appropriation. Stated another way, Diop's desire to prove Ramses was black was a futile exercise. Diop could not provide solid evidence that Ramses II was black, since this Pharaoh was in fact not black. In 1976, a group of French scientists working with the permission of the Egyptian government examined the mummy of Ramses II and concluded that the dead king was "a 'leucoderm,' that is, a fair-skinned man, like prehistoric or ancient Mediterraneans, or, perhaps, the Berbers of Africa."[188] The only Egyptian dynasty that could be called black without qualification, in the modern sense of the word, was the Kushite or Twenty-fifth Dynasty, 747–656 B.C.[189]

The Afrocentrists' obsession with race also extends to their discussion of ancient notables and royalty. This monomania is an example of Afrocentrism's intellectual sloth and inability to break out of the tradition of contributionist history that I discussed earlier. It also reflects Afrocentrism's inability to engage some of the criticisms of this genre in contemporary black American historiography.[190] Contributionist claims, for example, that Hannibal and Saint Augustine were black are naive in light of what we know today about reading race in the ancient world. Why then has Asante recently stated without qualification that "both Hannibal and Saint Augustine were Black Africans. No question about it"?[191] If Asante were more exacting in his research, he would be more cautious in his assertions. Hannibal was a Phoenician, one of a Semitic seafaring people who settled in North Africa. As a Romanized Berber, Saint Augustine did not think of himself as either black or African.[192] In claiming these men as black, Asante is not breaking new scholarly ground; he is simply serving up, without scrutiny, discredited theories from the nineteenth century.

The clearest expression of the Afrocentrists' need to claim

figures from antiquity as black can be seen in the controversy about Cleopatra VII's racial origins. While Mary Lefkowitz has correctly pointed out that Cleopatra was a Macedonian Greek, her correction of Afrocentrist claims about Cleopatra has been labeled by Asante and other Afrocentrists as "marginal" or "trivial." According to Asante, Lefkowitz "supports the dominant mythologies of race in the history of the West by diverting attention to marginal issues in the public domain."[193] Since the assertion of Cleopatra's blackness has been one of the mainstays of Afrocentric discourse, in disclaiming it, Asante has been forced to make statements that raise questions about his command of Afrocentric scholarship. "I can say without a doubt that Afrocentrists do not spend time arguing that either Socrates or Cleopatra were Black. I have never seen these ideas written by an Afrocentrist, nor have I heard them discussed in any Afrocentric intellectual forums."[194] However, both Yosef A. A. Ben-Jochannan and John Henrik Clarke have written extensively about the African origins of Western civilization and have labeled Cleopatra VII black. Ben-Jochannan, for example, incorrectly calls Cleopatra VII "Cleopatra VIII" and compounds his error by writing this nonsense: "Cleopatra VIII committed suicide after being discovered in a plot with Marc Antonio [Mark Anthony] to murder Julius Caesar."[195] This is a startling revisionist interpretation, in light of the fact that Julius Caesar had been dead for fourteen years when Cleopatra committed suicide. Clarke's analysis of Cleopatra is as problematic as Ben-Jochannan's; he too claims Cleopatra was black. "If she lived today," Clarke writes, "she would probably be classified as a light-skinned African-American."[196]

Although Cleopatra was queen of Egypt, Michael Grant has written that "she possessed not a drop of Egyptian blood in her veins."[197] Cleopatra's family, the Ptolemies, did not intermarry with their Egyptian subjects, and in fact Cleopatra was the only member of the family to speak Egyptian.[198] In claiming Cleopatra was black, the Afrocentrists have seized on the fact that she "had a fairly dark complexion."[199] "Her remote Macedonian forbears," Michael Grant says, "must have been of various complexions, since the Macedonians were of very mixed blood."[200] As a royal house, the Ptolemies married into the royal families of both Syria and Persia, and these alliances may have further darkened the family's complexion. This does not, however, make her "black," which as we have seen is an anachronism when applied to the ancient world. Nor does it validate Clarke's description of her as "light-skinned." The term "light-skinned" had no meaning in the world of Ptolemaic Egypt, where Cleopatra reigned. If Clarke means by "light-skinned" that Cleopatra was a "mulatto," "quadroon," or "octoroon," these taxonomies did not exist in Cleopatra's world.

Terms such as "mulatto" and "quadroon" are products of the New World slave systems of the seventeenth and eighteenth centuries. These categories were created to distinguish so-called authentic whites and authentic Negroes from those of mixed race, whose hybridity undermined the dichotomy of black and white. Miscegenation undermined the principle that all blacks were slaves and all slaves were black in the plantation complex of the New World. Categories such as "mulatto," "quadroon," or "octoroon" subverted the prevailing belief that there were pure races. In North America, the creation of these racial categories was subsumed under the "one drop rule" or law of "hypo-descent": one drop of black blood made a person black or negroid in the United States.[201] Madison Grant, an aristocratic American racist of the early twentieth century, expressed the idea underlying the law of hypo-descent thus: "the cross between a white man and a Negro is a Negro; the cross between a white man and a Hindu is a Hindu; the cross between any of the three European races and a Jew is a Jew."[202] This was not the view in the Caribbean or Latin America, where a more fluid process of racial designation operated. Thus, in calling Cleopatra "light skinned," Clarke is operating within the racist system his scholarship seeks to contest. Stated another way, Clarke and other Afrocentrists accept and further an ideology of racial categorization that is bankrupt.

The racialization of the ancient world has also led to other distortions of the past. This revisionism has to do with the role of monarchy in Africa or Egypt. In Egypt and Africa, the majority of the people were not royals. Moreover, it was only after 1789 that monarchies developed modern identities, as David Cannadine, Linda Colley, T. Fujitani, and A. J. Mayer have argued.[203]

In their discussion of royalty as a "black thing," the Afrocentrists are not alone. Malcolm X once wrote, "You and I were produced by kings and queens from the African continent."[204] Unfortunately the emphasis in Afrocentric discourse on monarchs has created a myth that everyone was a king or queen in Egypt or Africa. In black popular culture, this sensibility is captured in a song by the rap group Jungle Brothers:

My forefather was a king
He wore fat gold chains and fat ruby rings
Nobody believes this to be true
Maybe it's because my eyes ain't blue
You ain't gon' find it in your history book
Come here young blood and take a look
You dig down deep inside this hardcover
Don't you know that you was barred brother
All you read about is slavery
Never 'bout the black man's bravery
You look at the pictures and all they show is
AfriKan people with bones in their noses
That ain't true—that's a lie
You didn't get that from my lemon pie
Yea, I cut class, I got a "D"
Cause history meant nothin' to me.[205]

But if everyone was a monarch in this world, have we not lost those who occupied the subject position? Long before Her Britannic Majesty Elizabeth II proclaimed 1992 an *annus horribilis* because of a collapse of "family values" in the House of Windsor, royalty was a problematic construct. This point escapes the Afrocentrists in their celebration of Africa as a place of "origin for divine Kingship."[206] One only has to look at some of the eccentricities of royalty to see that this is a dubious concept of government to claim as part of one's cultural heritage. But since Afrocentrism does not contextualize ideas, personages, or events, this failing should not surprise us.

If black people need heroines, they probably can do without the example of Cleopatra or other members of the Ptolemaic dynasty. As queen of Egypt, Cleopatra practiced royal incest. She was the product of an incestuous marriage between her father and mother (who were brother and sister), and when she ascended the throne, she followed the tradition of Egyptian royalty and married two of her male siblings (in her case, half brothers) "in name at least," according to Michael Grant. This tradition of royal brother-sister marriage replicated the marriage of the Egyptian god Osiris to his sister Isis,[207] and—because incest in ancient Egypt was the prerogative of royalty—it reflected the fact that the pharaoh and his consort were considered living gods. The tradition of close family intermarriage also included occasional unions of fathers and daughters. Ptolemy IX, for example, having run out of sisters to serve as consorts, married his daughter Cleopatra Bernice III.[208] Cleopatra, it should be noted, also killed one of her consorts, Ptolemy XIV, and her half sister Arsinoe IV.[209] Moreover, the Ptolemies presided over a state that was grossly inegalitarian and undemocratic, whose principal population was peasant. "In Cleopatra's time," her biographer writes, "these fellahin probably numbered between seven and nine million [people and] a very large portion of this native population lived barely above subsistence level...wholly excluded from power."[210]

The major failing of Afrocentrism is not its preoccupation with ancient royalty, however, but a trivialization of black American history, Africa, and the black Atlantic that privileges the synchronic over the diachronic. The history of black people from Africa to America cannot be understood as a static phenomenon.

The historical transformation that produced the various *mestizáje* populations in the Americas undermines the claims Asante makes in this passage:

> Africalogy rejects the Africanist idea of the separation of African people as being short-sighted, analytically vapid, and philosophically unsound. One cannot study Africans in the United States or Brazil or Jamaica without some appreciation for the historical and cultural significance of Africa as source and origin. A reactionary posture which claims Africalogy as "African Slave Studies" is rejected outright because it disconnects the African in America from thousands of years of history and tradition. Thus, if one concentrates on studying Africans in the inner cities of the Northeast United States, which is reasonable, it must be done with the idea in the back of the mind that one is studying African people, not "made-in-America Negroes" without historical depth.[211]

Asante starts with a static, unchanging culture, which he then uses to claim that his critics are unhistorical. But culture is a process, not a static phenomenon, as Asante asserts here. What Asante dismisses as "made-in-America Negroes" are a people who, under trying circumstances, created a cultural system that sustained them through their travail as slaves.

Because Afrocentrism is silent about the context of slavery and the slave trade, Afrocentrists like Ron Karenga can make nonsensical statements like this: "The day the slave ship landed in America, our history ended and the white man's story began."[212] This assumes that blacks stopped being historical agents once they were brought to the Americas. It ignores the fact that most of the blacks taken to the Americas either had been slaves in Africa or had occupied some other dependent or subordinate position in African society. Precolonial Africa was not egalitarian, and the most common form of private property was slave property.[213] Since African slavery was not racial, as Nathan Huggins has noted, "the distinctions of tribe were more real to [Africans] than race."[214] Tribalism did not prevent Africans from selling members of their own tribes in order to satisfy the demand for slaves in the Americas. To do this, Africans subverted their own religious and legal institutions.

The participation of Africans in the slave trade negates the Afrocentrist claim that Africans have a special nature. According to one Afrocentrist, African values are "humanitarian rather than individualistic, spiritual and ethical rather than materialistic."[215] These are feel-good buzzwords that do not agree with the facts of African history. Nor can this problem be resolved by assertions such as "we are by...history, and conventions an African people" that do not deal with the problem of discontinuity that lies at the heart of African and black American history.[216] Asante goes so far as to write, "There are some people...who argue that Africans and African Americans have nothing in common but the color of their skin. This is not merely an error, it is nonsense. There exists an emotional, cultural, psychological connection between this people that spans the oceans and the separate existence."[217] "Facts are stubborn things," Lenin once wrote. The fact is that black Americans are people of African descent, not "Africans." Examination of the slave trade, Middle Passage, and dispersion of Africans in the Caribbean and North and South America indicates that Africans created hybrid cultures once they left their homeland.

The mutable nature of culture can be seen in *The Interesting Narrative of the Life of Olaudah Equiano or Gustavus Vassa the African,* published in 1789. Equiano was sold into slavery when he was about ten years of age. He came from the eastern region of modern-day Nigeria, and his language was Ibo. To read his narrative is to see how easily someone designated an African could lose his tribal culture. Equiano's first encounter with whites led him to think he was going "to be eaten by those white men with horrible looks, red faces and loose hair."[218] His fears were soon assuaged and he received a new name, learned English, and became a Christian. His resistance to everything but the name change was minimal.[219] As his fear of the "other" disappeared, the renamed Gustavus Vassa became comfortable in European culture.

> I now not only felt myself quite easy with these new country-men but relished their society and manners. I no longer looked upon them as spirits, but as men superior to us, and therefore I had the stronger desire to resemble them, to imbibe their spirit and imitate their manners; I therefore embraced every occasion of improvement, and every new thing that I observed I treasured up in my memory. I had long wished to be able to read and write, and for this purpose I took every opportunity to gain instruction, but had made as yet very little progress. However, when I went to London with my master I had soon an opportunity of improving myself, which I gladly embraced.[220]

Gustavus's conversion to Christianity produced a major reorientation in how he understood the world. Two examples will illustrate this point.

In some traditional African religions, time had only two dimensions—past and present. When Gustavus became a Christian, he added a new understanding of time to his life, that is, a belief in the future. According to Jon Sensbach, traditional African societies lacked "a concept of a future, because events in the future could not be known and therefore did not make sense. Time, then, did not move forward, but backwards through the generations and through history." In the world from which Gustavus came, "the past was the foundation for the present, and contained all the experience upon which community could base its decisions and its relations with God." African religions, in short, did not hold out to their adherents the possibility of a "messianic future" or "the hope of perfection in God's coming kingdom."[221] As a Christian, Gustavus now faced God as an individual. His new faith existed independently of a corporate base. Confronting God without the mediation of ancestors and community was a new experience for Gustavus. This had not been the case when he worshiped as an Ibo; in that tribal community, as in others, the quest for God was a community effort.[222]

Because he was a child and eager to learn, Gustavus easily adapted to the world of eighteenth-century England. Gustavus did not show the sort of remorse about the loss of his tribal past and religion that the Muslim slave Abou Bekir Sadiki expressed in the nineteenth century. Sadiki was sold to slave traders sometime during the first third of the nineteenth century and shipped to Jamaica. He lamented the loss of his Islamic world:

My parents' religion is of the Mussulman, they are all circumcised and their devotions are five times a day, they fast in the month of Ramadan, they give tribute according to their laws, they are married to four wives but the fifth is an abomination to them, they fought for their religion.…They don't eat meat except what they themselves kill. They do not drink wine nor spirits as it is held an abomination to do so. They do not associate with any that worship idols nor profane the Lord's name, nor do dishonor to their parents, or commit murder, or bear false witness, or who are courteous, proud, or boastful for such faults are an abomination unto any religion. They are particularly careful in the education of their children and in their behavior, but I am lost to all these advantages since my bondage I am corrupt.[223]

This quotation reveals the difficulty of maintaining cultural practices in a world where they had no meaning.

Sadiki's recollection of the world he lost is of a place governed by order, custom, and ritual. This world stands in sharp contrast to what Chaney Mack's father remembered of his life in Africa.

My father wuz a full-blooded African. He wuz about eighteen years old when dey brought him over. He come from near Liberia. He said his mother's name wuz Chaney, and dat's whar I gits my name. He said dar wan't no winter whar he come from, and if dey felt like it dey could all go stark naked. He wore a slip made of skins of wild animals that come down to his knees. When ships would land in Africa, de black folks

64

would go down to watch dem, and sometimes dey would show dem beads and purty things dey carried on de ship....

My daddy said in Africa dey didn't live in houses. Dey jest lived in de woods and et nuts and wile honey dey found in trees. Dey killed wile animals, skinned 'em and et 'em, but made slips out of de skins to wear demselves. Dey jest eat dem animals raw. Dey didn't know nothin' 'bout cooking. Dey even et snakes, but when dey found 'em dey cut deir heads off quick, 'fore day got mad and pizened demselves.

He said dey never heard 'bout God, and when dey died dey always bury dem at night. Dey dig a hole in de groun', and den everybody would git him a torch and march behind de two who wuz carrying de corpse to whar dey dug de grave. Dey didn't know anything 'bout singing and God. Dat was de last of dem.

Dey didn't make crops over dere. Dey jest lived on things dat growed on trees and killed wile animals. Ef dey got too hungry, dey would jest as soon kill each other and eat 'em. Dey didn't know any better.

When my daddy come over here, it went purty hard wid him having to wear clothes, live in houses, and work.[224]

Chaney Mack's father's description of life in Africa is hard to place in a tribal context. Did this African belong to an acephalous group? Or is his recollection of Africa the product of time, memory loss, and invention for his grandchildren in a new world? When read closely, the recollection conforms to the worst racist stereotype of Africa that could be imagined.

My point here is that removal from Africa was characterized by stress, adaptation, and deracination. It forced Africans to construct pasts that grounded them in some sense of community or place. This was their defense in the face of the horrors of the slave trade and Middle Passage. As Sidney Mintz has written, "The Atlantic slave trade may well have been the most colossal demographic event of modern times."[225] At the heart of this great forced movement of people lay a demographic disaster. "Between 1700 and 1774," Robin Blackburn writes, "half a million slaves were introduced to Jamaica, yet the slave population rose by only 150,000 between these two dates."[226] The center of this black catastrophe was the experience of Africans in the Caribbean, "where about one in four Africans died within the first three years of residence."[227] The vast loss of life that accompanied the slave trade and Middle Passage had a profound effect on African culture in the Caribbean and North and South America.

Once the Africans were removed from the social systems that gave cultural practices life, they had to change. This change had two sources: one came from the masters, who wanted their slaves to be sufficiently acculturated to do the work on their plantations; the other derived from the bondsmen themselves, who transformed their African cultures in order to survive in a new context.

Because it conceives of culture in essentialist terms, Afrocentrism cannot account for this process of change. The emphasis in Afrocentrist discourse on the African nature of black American culture "evades the empirical question of what really happened and masks the central theoretical issue of how cultures change," as Sidney Mintz and Richard Price have suggested.[228] Cultural change, I would argue, was essential to the Africans' survival in the Americas. They could not remain completely embedded in Africanity. Mastery of the dominant culture was an important strategy for survival. How, for example, would Frederick Douglass have been able to escape from slavery in Baltimore if he had not been able to "talk sailor like an old salt?"[229]

Mastery of not only English but also Anglo-American political ideology and Christianity supplied the slaves and free Negroes of North America with tools to resist their oppressors. The Gabriel revolt of 1800 in Virginia was deeply influenced by the ideologies of both the American and French revolutions.[230] In 1822, when the Denmark Vesey Conspiracy was uncovered, it was learned that participants were encouraged to resist their masters by a selective reading of the Bible. Denmark and his cohorts drew inspiration from the book of Revelation. Their plot also fused elements of African and Christian religion. The witch doctor Gullah Jack served as the medium for this process.[231] Even slaves newly arrived from Africa were attracted to the American idea of freedom. In 1863, Lieutenant Robert H. Isabelle, 2d Louisiana Native Guards [74th USCI], wrote that two privates, Wimba Congo and August Congo, had joined the company. These Africans had been in the United States only three years and had joined the Union Army to overthrow slavery.[232] The process of cultural transference was not solely white to black; recent studies of slavery show that the Africans brought skills from their homelands that enriched the material life of the colonies in the Americas.[233] These Africans were not so completely deracinated that they became zombies, as the Afrocentrist would have us think.

The mixture of peoples in the Americas was also physical. In the Caribbean and North and South America, new peoples emerged as a result of the mixture of African, Native American, and Caucasian blood.[234] These *mestizáje* populations confound the idea of a biologically or culturally pure African surviving into the late twentieth century. In the Caribbean and Latin America, the saying "money whitens" illuminates a world of racial mixture that challenges the American concept that one drop of black blood makes a person black. In Brazil, once mulattoes acquired the "education and civilized manners that upper class Brazilians deemed appropriate" they no longer were thought of as black. Writing in 1843, Count Alexis de Saint Priest of France commented on the Brazilian racial mosaic: "When I came here I thought I would find that mulattoes formed a class apart, rejected by whites and dominating blacks....[In reality they] are mixed, interfused with all [groups]; they are to be found among slaves, among the vilest of employments, but also among the high society and in the Senate."[235] In Colombia, a recent student of that country's Negro population has recorded a low level of racial identification. "Some Colombian blacks," Peter Wade observes, "don't identify themselves as blacks, and some mixed race people don't identify themselves with blacks."[236] When Henry Highland Garnet wrote in 1848 that "the Western world is destined to be filled with a mixed race," he was being prescient.[237] The very mixed nature of the population of the Americas undermines the idea of an African continuum, both culturally and biologically.

The conception of an African continuum is also contested by the fact that Africans in the Americas, who were more African than American, failed to overthrow slavery. Being "centered" in "Africanity" did not necessarily make these people more effective freedom fighters. In Jamaica, the Maroons, after some initial successes against the British, were forced to sign a treaty with their former masters. This treaty required the Maroons to return runaway slaves to the British. In short, the Maroons became slave catchers for their former masters.[238] The Maroons' alliance with the British was thus a pyrrhic victory. It did not give the Maroons the autonomy they desired. "The Maroons erred in relying too much on treaties," Michael Craton has written, "made with an inexorably expanding capitalism." Ultimately these treaties became "weapons of restraint" and, in the long term, undermined the independence of the Maroons.[239] The Maroons' relationship with whites, which involved both resistance and accommodation, was not unusual, given what we know about master-slave relations from a comparative perspective. What is surprising is how much these "freedom fighters" were resented by their peers who remained in bondage.

In Jamaica, for example, Michael Craton has noted that the Maroons were hated by the slaves: "The savage efficiency of their policing activities and the arrogant way they swaggered through plantations, making free with slaves, provisions, stock, and womenfolk" angered the bondspeople.[240] Underlying the Maroons' attitude toward the slaves was a contempt for those black people who "chose" not to resist their masters, Mavis Campbell has observed.[241] Even when the Maroons resorted to what Campbell has called an "inchoate pan-African argument," claiming that they were fighting the whites as a common enemy "to free all the slaves," this appeal was not persuasive, since the bondspeople remembered the Maroons' cooperation with their masters "to frustrate the thrust for freedom of those in servitude."[242] The memory of Maroon duplicity did not die out quickly in the British Caribbean. In 1865, blacks on the island of St. Thomas were heard to remark, "The Maroons sell out a part of the African that they may [be] free." These people also sang a song whose lyrics proclaimed, "Oh dem Maroon people a kill out me nation."[243] The word "nation" in this song indicates one of the major problems that confronted the Maroons.

Both Mavis Campbell and Monica Schuler have noted the failure of the Maroons to overcome or suppress the ethnic particularism that Africans brought to the West Indies. The African continuum that Afrocentrists celebrate as a sign of African resilience and vitality in the face of European oppression and cultural loss served as a brake on slave resistance within the Caribbean. Writing about the failure of West Indian slaves to develop a pan-African sensibility, Campbell says, "They encompassed a multiplicity of ethnicities, from different parts of the continent of Africa, with distinct linguistic affinities. Each ethnic group viewed itself as exclusive as a 'nation'—despite certain commonalities. The notion of a Pan-African solidarity was alien to their contemporary way of thinking."[244] Plagued by these differences, one leader of the Maroons insisted that his followers speak English to create a common language.[245] Nor are contemporary historians the only commentators on the cultural diversity of Jamaican slaves. Writing in the eighteenth century, Olaudah Equiano remarked on a visit to Kingston: "I was surprised to see the number of Africans, who were assembled together on Sundays....Here each different nation of Africa meet and dance, after the manner of their own country."[246] The problems that plagued the Maroons of Jamaica were shared by other slaves in the plantation complex who resisted their masters.

Brazilian Muslims who rebelled against slavery in 1835 were no more successful than their Jamaican cousins. These slaves "planned an African front that never materialized, even among neighboring nations who were culturally and linguistically related."[247] The historian of this revolt writes that the "rebels planned to take land, killing whites, cabras [i.e., "faded" blacks], Creoles, as well as any other blacks who might not side with them. They would keep the mulattos as their slaves and lackeys."[248] In brief, these rebels "did not envisage an egalitarian utopia," based on some pan-African sensibility.[249] Similar divisions also existed among the non-Muslim slaves of Brazil. Writing about these divisions, Eduardo Silva says, "Although they shared a similar social standing—and, indeed, because of this—the inhabitants of Little Africa also preserved the old discord of Africa itself: divided upon questions of different origins, customs and religions."[250] In Cuba, slave society was also riven by religious and ethnic lines.[251] In other words, consciousness of an African past did not necessarily lead to freedom. The Jamaican, Brazilian, and Cuban examples indicate the limitations of being "centered" in "Africanity" outside an African context. These cases show that neither color nor kinship alone was a sufficient basis for political action when the slaves chose to resist their oppressors violently. Writing in another context, David Potter nevertheless showed an understanding of this problem: "A sense of kinship is one thing, and an impulse toward political unity is another."[252]

The possibility of an "African continuum" becomes even more problematic when viewed against the history of free Negroes who went back to Africa in the nineteenth century. These people did not revert to tribal cultures. The gulf between repatriated Negroes and Africans was as wide as the chasm between blacks and whites in North America. This was also true of freed slaves sent back to Africa by the British. The early histories of both Liberia and Sierra Leone were marked by a great deal of strife and violence between black settlers and the indigenous people of the west coast of Africa. In Liberia, the Amero-Liberians created a society "based on privilege, they exaggerated real and subtle differences that distinguished them from the Bassa, Gola, Kru, Tiv, and Vai tribes occupying the grain-coast region of [Liberia].... They retained American tastes in food, dress, manners, and housing. They became fortresses of civilization amid the savages and the jungle."[253] Tellingly, American black settlers in Liberia were referred to by Africans as "whitemen."[254] Peyton Skipwith, writing from Liberia to his former master in 1840, articulated the feeling of difference that existed between Africans and American blacks: "In my present thinking if we have any ancestors they could not have been like these hostile tribes in this part of Africa for you may try and distill that principle and belief in them and do all you can for them and they still will be your enemy."[255]

Skipwith was not alone in thinking he was different from the local people. An emigré writing eight years later also commented on the Africans' enmity toward their putative American brothers.

"Tho I must say of a truth they are the most savage and blood thirsty people I ever saw or ever wish to see."[256] In claiming that some cultural connection exists between Africans and American blacks, Asante and other Afrocentrists repeat the error of Marcus Garvey, who also described as "African" black people living outside of Africa. Garvey did this, as I have written elsewhere, "because for him the race question was framed in terms of an unproblematically unified black identity, unfissured by differences and immune to determinants of...country."[257] According to Garvey, there was "absolutely no difference between the native African and the American and West Indian Negroes, in that [they are] descendants from one common family stock."[258] The people Garvey refers to here as "descendants [of] one common family stock" were in fact transformed by the historical processes of slavery, the Middle Passage, and acculturation.

In North America, this process of change meant that during the 1820s and 1830s free people of color began to drop the word "African" from the names of their schools and fraternal societies.[259] The only major black institutions that retained the term were the African Methodist Episcopal (A.M.E.) Church and the African Methodist Episcopal, Zion Church. The use of the word "African" in the A.M.E. Church's title, as one minister explained, did not mean "Methodism Africanized, nor Methodism from or for Africans only." He wrote, "The term expresses no fact as to accident of birth nor geographical position, yet it is significant in an ethnological sense. It expresses the fact that the church was founded, controlled by, and chiefly composed of persons of African descent, with African blood in their veins."[260]

In the nineteenth century, American blacks saw their history as an evolutionary process. The Reverend Alexander Crummell captured this sensibility in a sermon delivered at St. Mary's Chapel, in Washington, D.C., in 1877. "Indeed, the Negro, in certain localities, is a superior man, to-day, to what he was three hundred years ago. With an elasticity rarely paralleled, he has risen superior to the dreaded inflictions of a prolonged servitude, and stands, to-day, in all the lands of his Thralldom, taller, more erect, more intelligent, and more aspiring than any of his ancestors for more than two thousand years of a previous era."[261] In this context, black Americans saw themselves as having changed from African to Afro-American. In short, they had become a hybrid. "We are not Africans," one black leader proclaimed, "but a mixed race, mingling Saxon, Indian, and African blood."[262]

Among some American blacks, the process of acculturation resulted in a complete rejection of Africa: "The American Negro is no more African today than descendants of the Pilgrim fathers are Europeans; not as much, for...the Negro brought no civilization, hence took that which he found. He lost his heathenism and accepted Christianity, and in many cases became so intermingled until he has lost his color."[263] This sense of a transformed people was captured with great insight in the following quotation:

To say that we could preserve our African characteristics after dwelling for almost three centuries upon this continent, is most unphilosophical. Were it true we would be the most stolid race of the world—but whoever credited the Negro for stolidity. The fact is we are thoroughly Americans, and by reason of the fact that we have been here longer than the majority of the new American race, we have developed more fully than they, the characteristics by which it is to be known.[264]

Being an American black carried with it certain responsibilities in the late nineteenth century, including the duty to assume a vanguard position among the Negroes of the world. What I call here "Afro-Saxonism" was deeply rooted in the American ideas of exemplification and mission. If white Americans were the exemplar for the white world of the nineteenth century, "black Americans served the same function for their less advanced brothers."[265] The official newspaper of the African Methodist Episcopal Church, *The Christian Recorder,* made this point in an article published on November 21, 1868:

> Though still possessing in no little measure the deformed body and mean soul that slavery always makes, yet is the American Negro the best type of his race extant. Just as we regard the whites of America as possessing the noblest traits —traits which are yet to constitute them the leaders of their race, even so is it with the blacks.

In contrast, the Negroes of Brazil "who are still slaves, may be regarded as the lowest of our people on the American continent." The majority of these people, the paper said, "were doubtless born in Africa, and they have never thrown off its barbaric usages." The Negroes of the Danish West Indies, British West Indies, and Haiti were all deficient in character. In contrast to his less advanced brothers, the American Negro, having been raised and tutored in the house of Anglo-Saxonism, was a paragon of progress.

> The American Negro, unlike his brethren, has been the pupil of the cool, aspiring, all-conquering Saxon, and in no little measure he has partaken of all the greatness of his master. From him he has learned that form of government that is as surely destined to prevail the world over....From him he has received that type of Christian faith that tends to magnify the lowly of men....More than all, the American Negro has been close by the side of his white brethren, and has long seen how he applies these great principles—he has from example, learned the modus operandi of Republican government, of Protestant faith.[266]

In its efforts to root black people in an African worldview, Afrocentrism denies the multifaceted ways black Americans have identified with the United States. Writing thirty-five years ago, Le Roi Jones (later Amiri Baraka) commented on the irony of being both black and American. "The American Negro has a definable and legitimate historical tradition," Jones observed, "no matter how painful, in America, but is the only place such a tradition exists, simply because America is the only place the American Negro exists. He is, as William Carlos Williams said, 'a pure product of America.'"[267] The uniqueness of black American history, as Jones describes it, is a point that Afrocentrists ignore in their caricatures of black people, Africa, and America. "In a sense, history for the Negro before America," as Jones notes, "must remain an emotional abstraction. The cultural memory of Africa informs the Negro's life in America, but it is impossible to separate it from its American transformation."[268]

Finally, I want to argue that Afrocentrism is not history. To most contemporary historians, as Joan Scott has written, history "is an interpretive practice, not an objective natural science." Indisputably, an earlier generation of historians ignored Africa and black Americans as historical agents. Yet to claim that this continues to be the case today is to be disingenuous.[269] Thus, when Asante calls for a history that places "African ideals and values at the center of inquiry," he ignores the work of indigenous African historians such as K. O. Dike and others, who transformed the study of African history after World War II by placing Africans at the center of African historical inquiry. In doing this, these scholars gave Africans the voice they had lacked in British imperial history. In its refusal to credit African scholars with taking the lead in this process, Afrocentrism lacks an awareness of the research of others and shows an unwillingness to accept the fact that anyone, white or black, can think either systematically or skeptically about the past.[270]

If Afrocentrism is not history, what is it? Throughout this chapter I have called it a therapeutic mythology. I give it this description because of its emphasis on psychology. The problems of contemporary black Americans in Afrocentric discourse are conceptualized in terms of problems of the mind. Asante gives voice to this idea when he writes about the cultural and psychological confusion of blacks living outside Africa. "Of all the continents, Africa has often seemed the most disconcerted by its children who have been scattered over the globe. A great part of this has to do with the confusion of the children of Africa themselves. Often detached and isolated from Africa, they assume new identities and become doubly lost, zombies in the midst of stone and steel cities of the Americas." Asante attributes this psychological malaise to what he calls "menticide," defined as "the suicide of minds."[271] In making this claim, Asante echoes Marcus Garvey, Elijah Muhammad, Malcolm X, and the Maulana Ron Karenga, all of whom have argued that black Americans are psychologically incomplete. "We have always said," Karenga observes, "and continue to say, that the battle we are waging now is for the minds of black people."[272] In the struggle for black liberation, the mind is a big player. "There can be no freedom," Asante has written, "until there is freedom of the mind."[273] Asante's book *Afrocentricity* reads like a self-help book or psychological primer. When placed in the broader context of the contemporary recovery movement, it can only be called banal. Asante urges his readers to center themselves in a host of rituals that will result in a recuperation of "Africanity."[274] These include changes of name, dress, language, and religion, as well as "new thought."[275] Rather than being viewed as something new, Afrocentrism must be placed in a tradition of quasi-religious systems that developed in nineteenth-century America, techniques for self-improvement called "mind cure" and "new thought." Wendy Kaminer has defined these systems as "a loose collection of beliefs about mind power"[276] in which "you actually become what you think."[277] In "new thought," as in Afrocentrism, very little attention is paid to structures. What the Afrocentrists are concerned with when they talk about racism is attitudes, not racism's structural replication. Historically, black people were oppressed in America not because they lacked self-esteem but because they were black. Afrocentrism's obsession with antiquity dodges this issue. It differs therefore from the Universal Negro Improvement Association (UNIA) and the Nation of Islam, both of which have attempted to address the issue of black inequality by placing economic development at the center of their programs. But in a broader context, Afrocentrism's focus on the mind or self-esteem is conservative; its emphasis on individual transformation does not address broader issues of community or structural change. It only creates another class of exemplars in black society. This tactic or strategy makes Afrocentrism the enemy of a viable politics, that is, a politics that might do something about the unpleasant facts of contemporary black American life. Commenting on this form of black politics, the Black Panther newspaper on February 2, 1969, observed,

> Cultural nationalism manifests itself in many ways, but all of these manifestations are essentially grounded in one past; a universal denial and ignoring of the present political, social, and economic realities and concentration on the past as a frame of reference. These people usually want a culture rooted in African culture....In other words, cultural nationalism ignores the political and concrete, and concentrates on a myth and fantasy.[278]

Ultimately, Afrocentrism is about one thing—itself. In part 2, I will elaborate on the limits of "new thought" and self-esteem as techniques for racial revitalization.

79

In its efforts to recenter black Americans and improve black self-esteem, Afrocentrism has conjured up a host of demons. These "others" include Europe, Jews, gay people, and blacks who do not share the Afrocentric worldview, to name only a few. In Asante's defense, it must be noted that he does not express the rank anti-Semitism or the polygenetic racism ("ice people" and "sun people") formulation of Leonard Jeffries. Nor has Asante given voice to Frances Cress Welsing's theories about melanin as a sign of racial superiority.[279] Although he disavows the biological determinism of Jeffries and Welsing, Asante does talk about an "Afrocentric personality." This personality is biological or racial, and is defined as "African personalism." In Asante's paradigm, the West is materialistic and the East spiritual. In contrast, Africa combines both: "Personalism invades both the spiritual and the material. For us…the trees and the mountains have always possessed essences. We do not have to make absolute distinctions between mind and matter, form and substances, ourselves and the world. The self is the center of the world, animating it, and making it living and personal."[280] In its obsession with racial differences, Asante's Afrocentrism is blind to sociological and cultural differences. Thus Asante can say that "Paul Gilroy has a serious problem of racial identity. He can't decide whether he's black or British."[281] In Asante's world, one cannot be both black and British. Why is this the case? It has to do with the fact that Afrocentrism as a form of historical explanation is deeply grounded in that nineteenth-century racism I referred to earlier. The racism of the nineteenth century asserted that culture was a product of race; Afrocentrism does the same. In emphasizing essences and color,

Afrocentrism, like the "scientific racism" of the late nineteenth and early twentieth centuries, "views race as an immutable category, and history as a progression of racial civilizations."[282] Afrocentrism then stands in opposition to the black historical tradition I have called "contributionism," which was opposed to racism and was premised not on a biological conception of race but on a universal idea of humankind. In 1864, Frederick Douglass pointed out that the dignity of blacks should not depend on whether they were, or were not, the central actors in the history of antiquity.

> What if the Negro may not be able to prove his relationship to Nubians, Assyrians, and Egyptians? What if ingenious men are able to find plausible objections to all arguments maintaining the oneness of the human race? What, after all, if they are able to show very good reasons for believing the Negro to have been created precisely as we find him on the Gold Coast— along the Senegal and the Niger—I say, what of all this?— "A man's a man for a' that."…What, if we grant that the case, on our part, is not made out? Does it follow, that the Negro should be held in contempt?…I think not.[283]

PART TWO

"All God's Dangers Ain't a White Man,"

or "Not All Knowledge Is Power"

When southern sharecropper Nate Shaw observed, late in the nineteenth century, that "all God's dangers ain't a white man," he was talking about the boll weevil.[1] From our perspective a century or so later, however, we can see that the statement applies with equal force to a number of black spokesmen and leaders past and present, who, operating like beetles, have done and are doing damage to black America from within.[2] In this chapter I propose to take a closer look at the Afrocentrists by placing them in the context of their predecessors and by scrutinizing the dangers they pose to black America in the present era.

A rightward drift in American politics is moving the country back toward what I call "free market racism,"[3] the state of American race relations during the last quarter of the nineteenth century, when the ideology of laissez-faire reigned supreme in the realm of economics and race on the national level. Andrew Johnson's veto of the Freedmen's Bureau Bill of 1866 was the federal government's first step toward abandoning its position as a guarantor of Negro equality. In Johnson's veto message, Eric Foner has noted, the president "voiced themes that to this day have sustained opposition to federal intervention on behalf of blacks."[4] Following President Johnson's lead, the Supreme Court in the 1870s and 1880s reinterpreted the Fourteenth and Fifteenth Amendments and the Civil Rights Act of 1875 in a way that placed limits on federal authority in the enforcement of civil rights.[5] The Supreme Court's narrow interpretation of these laws delivered the freedmen back into the hands of their former masters. Ironically, the diminution of federal authority in the realm of black rights resulted in a highly regulated policing of race relations on the state level, especially in the South. It is in this context that Jim Crow emerged as the regnant mode of racial interaction in the United States in the 1890s.[6]

In contemporary America, having deregulated the economy, the federal government is also moving to create a society in which race relations on both the state and national levels will operate with minimal governmental interference. This is the meaning of phrases such as "a level playing field," "racial preferences," and "color-blind society," all of which reflect a degree of historical amnesia. As a historian of American race relations, I wonder if a society as color-conscious/color-phobic as this one can ever be color-blind. I say this, even though I do not think that race constitutes a site of profound and unbridgeable difference. I am also cognizant of the fact that I live in a country where most people continue to think that race is real.[7] I say this despite the American right's efforts to cloak its assault on affirmative action, for example, in universalist terms—that is, as a campaign against "racial preferences."[8]

Despite its claim to be color-blind, the campaign against affirmative action has been extremely racial or color-conscious, involving as it does the categorization of "black" as a marker of both incompetence and racial privilege through the use of coded language such as "merit," "reverse discrimination," and "racial preferences." Advocating color-blindness is a call for the maintenance of the racial status quo, since "color-blindness is not a fundamental principle of justice," as Amy Gutman has noted. The principle that should be guiding American race relations is "fairness."[9] By contrast, color-blindness is perfectly compatible with a society characterized by extreme racial inequality. The color-blind slogan or "level playing field" position ignores the inequitable impact of the law. In a color-blind society, a wealthy white man and a working-class black man are equal before the law, but they are not equal in terms of access or opportunity.

What color-blindness does is make the racial marker "white" exnominal. In other words, it makes normal what is assumed, not what is designated.[10] Color-blindness is a form of disavowal; it is a refusal to see, know, and comprehend difference. In short, although color-blindness is usually thought of as progressive and cosmopolitan, it is not. Instead, it maintains the authority of whiteness by reinscribing hierarchy and erasing diversity. Commenting on this point, a letter to the *New York Times* last year observed:

> For white Americans, being color-blind is supposed to be a sign of enlightenment and acceptance. But it also suggests a

hierarchical setting in which the group at the top deigns not to see something unsavory inherent in the group at the bottom. In short not seeing color is not a compliment to those who live daily with the effects of color nor, necessarily, a sign of having risen above the fray; it is an evasion.[11]

"White" in America has historically not been a racial category in American racial discourse in the same way that "Asian," "black," or "Latino" has been understood to be. This is a product of what scholars of "whiteness" see as its most notable attribute, that is, the inability of white people to see themselves as raced or racialized subjects.[12] As Ruth Frankenberg has written, whiteness in Euro-America "remains unexamined...essential, homogenous, seemingly self-fashioned, and apparently unmarked by history or practice (e.g., the notion of 'racial-ethnic communities' as synonym for 'communities of color')."[13] This kind of racialized myopia or denial has created the space in which the language of white victimhood referred to above operates with credibility. This language, in terms of the context of contemporary American racial politics, denotes or signifies white people as a socially disadvantaged group, for the second time in the history of the American republic. The first time this occurred was in President Andrew Johnson's veto of the Freedmen's Bureau Bill mentioned earlier.

Johnson labeled the bill racially preferential and therefore unfair to the interests of whites. "Congress has never felt itself authorized to spend money for renting homes for white people honestly toiling day and night, and it was never intended that freedmen should be fed, clothed, educated and sheltered by the United States. The idea upon which slaves were assisted to freedom was that they become a self-sustaining population."[14] What Johnson ignored in this message was that the freedmen had been slaves, who had never had the opportunity of "honestly toiling day and night" for themselves. The president's speech was also ironic in that it ignored the Homestead Act of 1862, which overwhelmingly benefited white farmers by enabling citizens or prospective citizens of the United States to claim 160 acres of public land. Claimants were required to pay a small fee after living on their property for five years. Since most black people in 1862 were either slaves or poor free Negroes unable to exercise this option, the Act's major benefactors were white yeomen. Johnson therefore was disingenuous in his veto of the Freedmen's Bureau Bill, since the government had been an active agent in the promotion of white social mobility from the time of the creation of the republic.

Johnson's defense of white privilege carried over into his veto of the Civil Rights Bill of 1866. The president wrote:

> In all our history, in all our experience as a people living under Federal and State law, no such system as that contemplated by the details of this bill has ever before been proposed or adopted. They establish for the colored race safeguards which go infinitely beyond any that the General Government has ever provided for the white race. In fact, the distinction of race and color is by the bill made to operate in favor of the colored and against the white race.[15]

Negroes were not "free" in the sense that whites were in the postbellum United States, despite the passage of the Thirteenth, Fourteenth, and Fifteenth Amendments to the Constitution. The nineteenth-century agitator and reformer Wendel L. Phillips understood the problematic nature of black freedom when he remarked that President Lincoln's Emancipation Proclamation "frees the slave but ignores the Negro."[16] Governmental interest in the freedmen received the coup de grace in 1883, when the Supreme Court declared the Civil Rights Act of 1875 unconstitutional. The majority opinion in this case proclaimed that blacks should stop being "the special favorite of the law."[17]

Like President Johnson and the Supreme Court of the late nineteenth century, contemporary critics of affirmative action either are blind or choose to ignore the fact that black people today are the heirs to long-term structural inequality,[18] a problem that, as Supreme Court Justice Ruth Bader Ginsburg has noted, continues to be "evident in our work places, markets and neighborhoods."[19] These issues should be at the center of any discussion of affirmative action, but they are not. Instead, the right uses terms like "racial preference," conflating affirmative action with Jim Crow, an ugly period of American history that some Americans, black and white, seem to have forgotten or think is behind them. Under Jim Crow, racialized subjects regardless of their color, class, education, or gender were excluded from equal opportunity. White fears of affirmative action, I would suggest, embody the problematic nature of whiteness in the twenty-first century.[20] That is, a loss of privilege based on color.

Black spokesmen have vociferously denounced the rollback of

affirmative action and other retreats on the civil rights front. But civil rights organizations need to devote as much energy, as Bob Herbert has written, "to enemies within."[21] "Enemies" may be too strong a word to use in this context, but it does capture the fact that the Afrocentrists and other black nationalists since the collapse of the civil rights movement have filled a void in black cultural and political life. Chanting the mantra of essentialized blackness, the Afrocentrists represent a decline in the quality, style, and vision of an earlier generation of black spokespeople. Professor Cornell West captured the limitations of present-day black leaders when he wrote, "Martin, Ella, and Fannie made sense of the black plight in a poignant and powerful manner, whereas most contemporary black political leaders' oratory appeals to black people's sense of the sentimental and sensational."[22]

As I indicated in part I, Afrocentrism sentimentalizes Africa by depicting it as a place where blacks lived in perfect harmony before the arrival of whites. Like the Puritan "city on a hill," the Afrocentrists' Africa is a transhistoric exemplar. Its "sensational" place within this cultural paradigm resides in the racialization of ancient personages and the naming of Africa as the ur-site of Western civilization. Underlying these propositions is a therapeutic aim to get black Americans to appreciate the real unity of their history and to adopt a particular narrative account of that past. The philosopher Brian Fay calls this act of self-realization "self-clarity," which he defines as "a group learning the genuine narrative of its life in which all its significant events are placed in their proper order, and in which the immanent direction of its genuine satisfaction is revealed."[23] Operating as false "self-clarity" within the black community, Afrocentrism is based on a racial essentialism and an underlying presumption that even if all black people do not look alike, they should think alike because it is in some form of group thought that American Negroes will find redemption. I will return to this point later on. Finally, Afrocentrism is a ritualistic invocation of community as the site or origin of racial authenticity: black people are nothing if they do not identify with the community. This was one of the messages purveyed at the Million Man March,[24] which also reflected contemporary black thinking about community in that it was a man's affair.[25] Black women were excluded from this event because the crisis of community in black America today, as perceived and articulated by Minister Farrakhan and others, is a problem of black men. Farrakhan told the crowd attending the march, "Clean up, black men, and the world will respect and honor you. But you have fallen down like the prodigal son and you're husking corn and feeding swine…with the filth of degenerate culture."[26] The defect that the minister describes can be "repaired by intervening in the family to compensate and rebuild the race by instituting appropriate forms of masculinity and male authority."[27] The current use of the language of community and family in black America, as Paul Gilroy and Adolph Reed have both argued, is authoritarian and reactionary,[28] reflecting not only a fear of collapsed boundaries between black men and women but also an anxiety about the future of black culture, institutions, and even the category "black" itself. Indeed, discomfort about racial integration and its impact on black people is shared by Afrocentrists and integrationists alike. The origins of their dread about the future of what I call "black" emanates from different philosophical and political positions, however.

For Molefi Kete Asante, integration has caused blacks to commit menticide, "the suicide of minds."[29] It has encouraged American Negroes to pursue activities that are incompatible with Afrocentric values. "Why should we excel, be integrated or work? There is no reason for any of these tactics unless they worked toward the profound Afrocentric objective."[30] Bell hooks, doyen of multiculturalism, thinks social integration "has had a profound impact on black gender roles. It has helped to promote a climate wherein most black women and men accept sexist notions. Unfortunately, many changes have occurred in the way black people think about gender....For example: to what extent did the civil rights movement, with its definition of freedom as having equal opportunity with whites, sanction looking at white gender roles as a norm black people should imitate?"[31] Just what impact the civil rights movement had on black gender roles is unclear. What is clear in hooks's explanation, however, is demonization. That is, the changes, if any, in black gender roles are explained in terms of some external agent, in this case, white hegemony. Unfortunately for hooks, there is no empirical evidence to substantiate her assertions.

A more reasoned, nuanced, and grounded assessment of the impact of integration on Negro life is provided by Gerald Early in his moving book *Daughters*. In a section entitled "A Racial Education," Early reminisces about the impact of his success in an integrated world on his wife and daughters. Although he does not pine for segregation, there is a sense that integration has cost black people something.[32] In a number of black middle-class homes this anxiety is expressed in a foreboding that black children growing up in integrated neighborhoods will lose an awareness of the culture that shaped the lives of their grandparents and parents. One friend of mine recently complained to me that her sons had black friends who had never heard of Ralph Ellison or Richard Wright. I told her that in my teaching I have had black students who did not know what either "Juneteenth" or the Emancipation Proclamation were. This fear of cultural loss is pervasive within highly educated members of the black middle class. But anxiety about the future of black culture and black people also exists among a number of blacks not formally educated. Grandparents, as Early reports, often tell their successful children that their kids are growing up not knowing black people, advising that "you had better expose these kids more to black folk and get ''em out of the suburbs.'"[33] Accompanying this unease are anxieties about interracial dating and sex. "What will happen to the race," a friend of my late stepmother's once asked me, "if our brighter young people marry whites?" Just as the twin processes of social mobility and movement to the suburbs have alienated many white families from a sense of their heritage, integration has been a problematic experience for some black people.[34]

The reservations expressed about integration by Early, hooks, and the people whose conversations I've reported do not, I believe, represent a nostalgia for segregation. Asante's position is less straightforward, however, because his Afrocentrism, despite its claim to be a radical contestation of Western hegemony, is really a late-twentieth-century expression of accommodationism.

Afrocentrism, as I argued in part 1, is an effort on the part of its proponents to create a heroic space for American Negroes that will give them a semblance of intellectual and psychological equality with or superiority to whites. It also involves a retreat from Western instrumentalism (otherwise known as "reason") into racial romanticism and thus is reactionary. I call this accommodation because, like Booker T. Washington's program, it involves the creation of a space for black people where, in theory, they can live free of white authority. Afrocentrism, in short, is a central component in the creation of a false sense of community. Instead of viewing the current emphasis in black America on community, self-help, and the emergence of new leaders as unique or as an aberration, we must place these developments in the broad sweep of black American history, particularly the history of blacks as it unfolded after 1877.

In an important book published in the 1960s and titled *Negro Thought in America, 1880–1915*, the historian August Meier adumbrated a theory that explained shifts in black thought during the last quarter of the nineteenth century and first decade of the twentieth. I quote Professor Meier at some length because his analysis is relevant to a number of the issues I am discussing here. According to Meier:

The changing outlook of Negroes took a number of different forms. If the Republican party was becoming indifferent toward Negroes, a few thought it would be profitable to divide their votes and form a balance of power between the two major parties. If Republican indifference and Southern disenfranchisement closed off political avenues of advancement, then economic and moral development should be the area for endeavor. If whites grew more hostile to Negroes, then Negroes must help themselves and band together to advance their cause. If whites believed Negroes to be inferior, then Negroes must show themselves to be the equals of whites—by publicizing their past achievements, by successfully running the race of Social Darwinist competition with the whites, and by cultivating a vigorous racial pride to offset the "Anglo-Saxon consciousness of kind." If whites did not want to bother with Negroes, then, many believed, it would be best to form their own segregated institutions and communities, or even emigrate to Africa. But above all, Negroes must stick together and help themselves.[35]

In this passage Meier is describing the collapse of Reconstruction. In the aftermath of this experiment in racial transformation, American blacks turned to self-help and community development. Politics, blacks had learned, was white men's business and therefore dangerous for them to participate in. As Meier goes on to note, this frame of mind was not new, having occurred twice before. The first time came in the wake of the Revolutionary era, when there was what Meier calls a "conservative reaction" and blacks turned inward to create a number of racial institutions. The most notable of these was the African Methodist Episcopal Church, which was organized in 1816. The second time came during the sectional crisis of the 1850s, when emigrationism became popular among American blacks.[36]

The United States is not reverting to de jure segregation, as in the past. What I want to suggest, nevertheless, is that for many black Americans the current direction of race relations bears an uncanny resemblance to past events and has thus produced a response reflecting earlier calls for "self-help, racial solidarity, and economic development as better techniques for racial advancement than politics, agitation, and the demand for immediate integration."[37]

The popularity of these ideas can be seen in one of the major issues discussed at the Million Man March. During the march, Minister Farrakhan told the assembled black male crowd, "If we start clothing the black community with business, opening up factories, challenging ourselves to be better than we are, white folk, instead of driving by, using the 'N' word, they'll say...'we can't say they're inferior anymore.'"[38] Minister Farrakhan here echoes the message preached in the last quarter of the nineteenth century by a number of black spokesmen, including the newspaperman and radical T. Thomas Fortune, the educator Booker T. Washington, and the Baptist preacher, missionary, and historian George Washington Williams.[39] Fortune, for example, thought that the problems of Southern blacks would disappear as the former slaves made economic progress. "When the lowly condition of the blackman has passed away; when he becomes a capable president of banks...when he has successfully metamorphosed the condition which attaches to him as a badge of slavery and degradation, and made a reputation for himself as a financier... his color will be swallowed up in his reputation, as in his bank-account and his important money interest."[40] Fortune was not alone in thinking that black enterprise would solve the race problem. George Washington Williams, echoing Fortune, wrote, "And if the Negro is industrious, frugal, saving, diligent in labor, and laborious in study, there is another law that will quietly and peaceably, without a social or political shock, restore him to his normal relations in politics."[41] The idea that if blacks were hardworking and frugal they would succeed in America became a central component of black thought in the last quarter of the nineteenth century, so much so that the graduating class of Tuskeegee Institute in 1886 chose as its class motto the slogan "There Is Room at the Top."[42] The students' boosterism reflected the opinion of their principal, Booker T. Washington, who, as the foremost spokesman of black America after Frederick Douglass died in 1895, was the chief architect of racial accommodation. Self-help and withdrawing from politics were crucial elements in Washington's plans for fin de siècle Negro America. Writing in 1899, Washington had the following to say about self-help:

> Nothing else so soon brings about right relations between the two races in the South as the industrial progress of the negro. Friction between the races will pass away in proportion as the black man, by reason of his skill, intelligence, and character, can produce something that the white man wants or respects in the commercial world. This is another reason why at Tuskegee we push the industrial training. We find that as every year we put into a Southern community colored men who can start a brickyard, a sawmill, a tin-shop, or a printing-office,—men who produce something that makes the white

man partly dependent upon the negro, instead of all the dependence being on the other side,—a change takes place in the relations of the races. Let us go on for a few more years of knitting our business and industrial relations into those of the white man, till a black man gets a mortgage on a white man's house that he can foreclose at will. The white man on whose house the mortgage rests will not try to prevent that negro from voting when he goes to the polls. It is through the dairy farm, the truck garden, the trades, and commercial life, largely, that the negro is to find his way to the enjoyment of all his rights. Whether he will or not, a white man respects a negro who owns a two-story brick house.[43]

What neither Farrakhan nor Washington makes explicit in their celebration of capitalism as the answer to the nation's racial problems is that black capitalism cannot be created by either rhetoric or hard work. Stated another way, capitalism is a product of capital, and in both the nineteenth and twentieth centuries black people lacked capital.[44] But there was and is another problem inherent in these spokesmen's injunctions to black people, namely, that peace may not ensue from a program of economic self-help. Certainly this was the lesson that Booker T. Washington's most zealous adherents learned late in the nineteenth century. Their program of embourgeoisment was fraught with difficulties and violence. Over the course of fifty-seven years (1889–1946), close to 4,000 Negroes were lynched, a number of them successful practitioners of Washington's philosophy.[45] What underlay the violence directed at these black people was the belief on the part of some whites that they were out of their place. When placed in a broader context, the discrimination and terrorization directed at black people in the United States was part of a worldwide process that also affected emancipated racialized populations in Africa, Europe, and Latin America.[46] Self-help, in short, was not the cure-all its nineteenth-century proponents thought it was.

Although self-help is an important component of the reorientation of present-day black political and social strategies, accompanying this process is a call for a more positive history, one that depicts black people as achievers and not ciphers. On a number of American college campuses this desire is manifested in some black students' call for a history that ignores slavery. They want to know instead what black people were like before their enslavement and the Middle Passage, thus following the Afrocentric agenda of denial or silence about African slavery and the role that bondspeople in general played in traditional African society. To get around the issue of indigenous African slavery, the Afrocentrists have invented an African world we have lost, in which all social relations took place between equals. Africans in America are described by Afrocentrists not as "slaves" but as "enslaved" (perhaps a more appropriate description of their situation would be "freedom-impaired"), thus indicating that prior to the Atlantic slave trade there was no bondage in Africa.[47] The use of the euphemism "enslaved" is a form of reality rupture. It reflects a shame in being descended from bondspeople and tries to make palatable something that was not nice. The historian James Horton, commenting on this state of mind, has remarked, "Now today, a lot of blacks feel we shouldn't use the term 'slave.' We should talk about 'enslaved people,' which they think is somehow less shameful. But that's prettifying slavery in the same way slaveholders did when they referred to 'my family' or 'my people.' Slavery wasn't a part-time job. It was a full-time thing, and we have to face its ugliness squarely."[48]

Further, the forced nature of the removal of Africans from Africa raises questions about the use of the word "diaspora" in contemporary discourse.[49] As currently used by mainstream scholars and particularly by Afrocentrists, the word "diaspora" obscures more than it reveals. The original diaspora was the dispersal (actually several dispersals) of the Jews from the Holy Land by Gentile conquerors. There is perhaps some parallel here with the black African experience in the sense that both peoples were forced to leave their homelands, but there are obvious and enormous differences between expulsion and captivity that make the comparison unhelpful. Even less fruitful is the attempt to connect the African slave experience with what have come to be called "diasporas" of various groups who emigrated in large numbers from their homeland. African slaves, after all, were a commodity and not agents of their own history. No African volunteered to come to the Americas to work. The history of Africans in the New World thus differs from, say, the history of the Germans or Irish in North America. There is no analog here to the African slave trade. Finally, the use of the word "diaspora" prettifies an ugly process, the slave trade, which after all constitutes an important moment in the history of Africa, the Americas, and capitalism. Like the Afrocentrists' insistence on talking of "enslavement," the use of the word "diaspora" effaces this historical reality.[50]

In calling for a more positive history, today's black people are echoing similar demands made in the last decade of the preceding century by E. A. Johnson, a black businessman and educator in North Carolina. Johnson had this to say of history: "It must, indeed, be a stimulus to any people to be able to refer to their ancestors as distinguished in deeds of valor, and particularly so to the colored people…a race of people once the most powerful on earth.[51] Underlying Johnson and others' focus on history was a belief that knowledge of a positive past would play an important role in shaping the psyche of black people. According to D. A. Straker of South Carolina, the history of blacks had to be taught in a special way: "There is enough history of the Negro race to make a Negro proud of his race.…why not then teach the Negro child more of himself and less of others, more of his elevation and less of his degradation? This can produce true pride of race, which begets natural confidence and unity."[52] In the early part of the twentieth century Carter G. Woodson, in a more nuanced fashion, called for a black history that would "set forth what the race has thought and felt and done as a contribution to the world's accumulation of knowledge and the welfare of mankind."[53]

Uniting all of these calls for a positive history was the belief that history has a therapeutic purpose. But we study the past neither to feel good nor to feel bad about ourselves. Historians study the past to understand the past, and they do this with the awareness that a positive history does not prevent people from committing horrible crimes or making mistakes. In the twentieth century the histories of Germany, Japan, and the former Yugoslavia illustrate this point.[54] This is a problem often ignored in contemporary discussions of history in black America, particularly within the Afrocentric movement. The stated purpose of Afrocentric history is to correct the condition of "menticide" or anomie affecting black people that has caused them to lose touch with their roots or Africanness. The Afrocentric cure-all for this psychic defect is education, and in Afrocentric education, history (or, more precisely, the romantic and selective version of the past that Afrocentrists construe as history) plays an important role.[55] According to Maulana Karenga in his book *Introduction to Black Studies,*

> the core task of Black Studies [read Afrocentrism]…freeing both Black history and humanity from alien hands, and reconstruction is a theoretical and practical project.…For to rescue Black history is not only to free it from denial, deformation and destruction academically, but also to free it socially from the same negatives by freeing the people who are both its producers and products. Likewise, the reconstruction of Black history demands intervention not only in the social process to reshape reality in Black images and interests and thus, self-consciously make history.…For history is the substance and mirror of a people's humanity in other's eyes as well as in their own eyes. It is, then, not only what they have done, but also a reflection of who they are, what they can do, and equally important what they can become as a result of the past which reveals their possibilities.[56]

Karenga is not alone in calling for a new or reconceptualized version of history. The late William Leo Hansberry, professor of history at Howard University, thought that "blacks should commit themselves more fully to the writing of their own history" because "black students need an Afrocentric perspective of their history."[57] John Henrik Clarke gives voice to this same paranoia when he writes that

> Europeans have presented an image of themselves to the world that is the image of the achiever, of the problem-solver, the hero—the image of success. This menticide, this conquest of the Afrikan mind and the mind of most of the world's people, is Europe's greatest achievement. I call this "the manifestation of the evil genius of Europe." An inadequate people, a bunch of overgrown juvenile delinquents, took over the world and convinced a whole lot of their victims that they had a *right* to do it, that it was good for the world to let them do it. They decided that Europe was their home. Enclaves like Canada and the United States were their homes outside of Europe. The rest of the world was their servants' quarters.[58]

Karenga, Hansberry, and Clarke are trying to create what Nietzsche called a posteriori or new history. In Nietzsche's words this is "an attempt to give oneself, as it were *a posteriori*, a past in which one would like to originate in opposition to that in which one did originate."[59] Afrocentrism does this when it claims Egypt as a black civilization and ignores both the acephalous and organized societies of West Africa from which most North American slaves originated, the ancestors of contemporary black Americans. By focusing on Egypt,

Afrocentrism only replicates the old Imperial school of history, which conceived of ancient Egypt as the only site of civilization in Africa because it had a written language. This was bad history—selective in its purview, racist in its argument, and didactic in its intent. It told its readers what they wanted to think and thus, like Afrocentrism today, it posed no challenge to the racial status quo. Revisionist history, to be valid, must critically interrogate source material and posit a creditable interpretation based on solid evidence, ideally evidence that is cross-referenced and drawn from a wide range of sources. In addition, good revisionist history must move beyond mere assertion to suggest an alternative interpretation. Unfortunately, Afrocentric history meets none of these criteria. A close examination of a few Afrocentric pronouncements will serve to illustrate this point.

For example, what is to be made of Molefi Kete Asante's assertions about Booker T. Washington? According to Asante, "Washington's sacrifice for the educational, economic, and political advancement of his people took the greatest sagacity and courage of his era."[60] Asante's assessment of Washington was not shared by Nate Shaw, an Alabama sharecropper and contemporary of the Wizard. Commenting on Washington, Shaw had the following to say:

> He was a nigger of this state and well known and everything, but here's what his trouble was, to a great extent: he didn't feel for and didn't respect his race of people enough to go rock bottom with em. He leaned too much on the white people that controlled the money—lookin out for what was his worth,

that's what he was lookin for. He was a big man, he had authority, he had pull in life, he had a political pull any way he turned and he was pullin for Booker Washington. He wanted his people to do this, that, and the other, but he never did get to the roots of our troubles. He had a lot of friends, he had a lot of courage, but it was all his way. He had a lot of anything a man needed for hisself, but the right main thing, he weren't down with that. Yet and still the veil was over the nigger's eyes. Booker Washington didn't try to pull that veil away like he shoulda done. He should have walked out full-faced with all the courage in the world and realized, "I was born to die. What use for me to hold everything under the cover if I know it? How come I won't tell it, in favor of my race of people? Why would I not care who sinks just so I swim?" Wrong-spirited. Booker Washington was—quite natural, there's nobody on earth perfect, but Booker Washington was a man got down with his country in the wrong way.[61]

The disaffection that some Southern black peasants felt toward Washington is a subject that American historians have not examined in detail—an unfortunate omission, since members of the black intelligentsia cannot have been Washington's only critics. Appropriating Washington for ideological reasons, Asante writes, "As a young man he made an Afrocentric commitment to the black people of Alabama."[62] This statement will come as a surprise to anyone who has read Washington's memoir *Up from Slavery*, since the book has very little positive to say about the autochthonous culture of southern black peasants.

Washington was a black Victorian who wanted to still the laughter of his people and make them black Yankees. He had very little sympathy for either Africans or African culture. Washington expressed his concern for the Africans by sending students from Tuskegee to work for the government of Kaiser Wilhelm II in Togo.[63] In South Africa he "urged that Africans be taught English in order to give them a common language and to absorb them more fully into Western culture."[64] As a member of the Congo Reform Association, Washington subscribed to the idea that Great Britain was engaging in a "civilizing mission" in Africa. If Washington was an Afrocentrist, should we conclude that Afrocentrism was and is complicit in the "civilizing" of the British Empire?[65]

In all fairness to Asante, it must be said that he is not alone in making these kinds of absurd statements. In a similar spirit, John Henrik Clarke has observed of precolonial Africa that it was characterized by "sharing societies....In many of these societies, most of them, there was no rich or poor."[66] The vision of Africa posited by Clarke is of a world not riven by "famine, disease, political insecurity, and economic miscalculation."[67] Clarke's perspective on precolonial Africa is utopian, not historical, an idealization of the past. It also represents a return to an earlier tradition of black discourse about Africa that attempted to counter white American charges that blacks, whether slave or free, had come from a savage land. The Reverend Peter Williams, in an oration delivered in 1808, described Africa before the arrival of Europeans as a place where no prince ever "unsheathed his sword, but in the cause of justice."[68] Similar encomiums to Africa were delivered in 1809 by Henry Sipkins: "But O! Africa, thou first fair garden of God's planting, thou once delightful field and original nursery for all those delicious fruits, tasteful herbage, and fragrant plants, that man highly prises [sic], thou track of earth over which the blest luminary, the sun, delights to make his daily splendid pass, thou spot of earth."[69]

Both Williams's and Sipkins's utopianism can be explained in that they were working within the tradition of contributionist black history, the source of their romantic picture of Africa. These nineteenth-century black men did not have the benefit of modern history and anthropology, both of which now provide a more complex understanding of the African past and social organization. John Henrik Clarke and other Afrocentrists have had the opportunity to consult this body of work, however. Their failure to do so has perpetuated in certain circles of black America an image of Africa that is irresponsible. Even when African intellectuals point out to Afrocentrists that their understanding of Africa is incorrect, they are met with hostility. Professor K. Anthony Appiah reports that when an African scholar told some Afrocentrists their construction of Africa was incorrect he was told, "We do not need you educated Africans coming here to tell us about African culture."[70] How do we explain this willful ignorance?

The best explanation I have seen so far has been provided by Taleb K. Mouhamed, a Mauritanian scholar teaching at Boston University. "For African Americans," Mouhamed says, "Africa is *the origin* an unknown. For most, it is voluntarily unknown." According to Mouhamed, this process involves black Americans who wish to remain ignorant of Africa and those who become fanatical on the subject of Africa and suffer reality rupture.[71] John

Henrik Clarke and his peers have constructed within the febrile interstices of their imaginations an Africa that never was. Take, for example, the Afrocentrist conception of Africa as an egalitarian paradise.

Social stratification was a central component of African life. As in other societies, class told people who they were and were not. One of the more interesting categories of social dependency in both precolonial and colonial Africa was pawnship, a supplement to the slavery that, as previously noted, was widespread in African society. Pawns were freeborn Africans—men, women, and children—who were indentured in lieu of payment of interest on a debt.[72] Writing in the eighteenth century, Mungo Park, the first white man to reach the interior of Africa, described interaction between an African ruler and his subjects:

> Every evening during my stay I observed five or six women come to the Mansa's house, and receive each of them a certain quantity of corn. As I knew how valuable this article was at this juncture, I inquired of the Mansa whether he maintained these poor women from pure bounty, or expected a return when the harvest should be gathered in. "Observe that boy," said he (pointing to a fine child about five years of age); "his mother has sold him to me for forty days' provision for herself and the rest of her family."[73]

Informed scholarship about Africa notes that not all Africans were satisfied with their traditional societies. For Africans who became Christians the new religion was, for example, a source of liberation. "With the majority of the converts Christianity was a political deliverer. It is essential to note that while there was happiness and contentment to a considerable degree," the Nigerian historian E. A. Ayandele has written, "in the traditional society there were certain aspects of tribal government and laws, which the common people did not like, but which they had to submit to because of tribal sanctions imposed by indigenous religion, customs, chiefs and 'public opinion.' For traditional society was by no means egalitarian, and acts of oppression of the common people by chiefs and the privileged few, such as exactions of produce and travesties of justice, did occur, although the extent varied from locality to locality."[74] If the Afrocentrists were truly concerned with what black Americans thought about Africa, they would teach Ayandele's interpretation of tribal society. "Any attempt to claim for the tribal society that all was pleasant for the common people," Ayandele says, "would be a romantic rather than objective analysis of the state of things."[75] Would be, and unfortunately —as far as the Afrocentrists are concerned—is.

The fact that Africa was not egalitarian does not mean it was either bad or inferior, only human and different. The Afrocentrists, however, are content with nothing less than perfection, as they construe it. We must therefore see the Afrocentrist construction of Africa as an ideal type, and therefore an integral part of the process that Franz Fanon, writing in another context, described as the "liberation of the man of color from himself."[76] Unfortunately for the Afrocentrist, this endeavor has not been very successful because, as Ranajit Guha has reminded us, no "discourse can oppose a genuinely uncompromising critique to a ruling culture so long as its ideological parameters are the same as those of that very culture."[77] But the problem of contestation becomes even more difficult if the contestors do not understand the history or culture of the people they are contesting. Afrocentrism's construction of Europe is framed around the same "unanimism" that informs its understanding of Africa. The idea of Europe in Afrocentric thought is not contingent, it is essential.[78]

This problem is most apparent in efforts by Afrocentric scholars to demystify Europe as a site of superior human achievement. Among black nationalists, the Afrocentrists are not the first to do this. Marcus Garvey, for example, depicted the Continent and its people as both parasitical and backward in his poem, "The Tragedy of White Injustice":

> Out of cold old Europe these white men came,
> From caves, dens and holes, without any fame,
> Eating their dead's flesh and sucking their blood,
> Relics of the Mediterranean flood;
> Literature, science and art they stole,
> After Africa had measured each pole,
> Asia taught them what great learning was,
> Now they frown upon what the Coolie does.[79]

Malcolm X, in his pamphlet *On Afro-American History*, makes similar claims about Europe. "In that day," Malcolm says, "the Black man in Egypt was wearing silk, sharp as a tack, brothers. And those people in Europe didn't know what cloth was. They admit this. They were naked or they were wearing skins from animals. If they could get an animal, they would take his hide and throw it around their shoulders to keep warm."[80] What unites the Afrocentric, Garvey, and Malcolm X perspectives on Europe is a failure to critically interrogate the sources that claim that the Europeans lived in caves.

Afrocentrists' characterization of the continent as backward derives not from African sources but from ancient histories of Rome. Descriptions of the Britons, Gauls, and Germans as backward, skin-wearing people may be found in both Julius Caesar's *The Conquest of Gaul* and the works of Tacitus. Caesar, for example, writing about the Britons, had the following to say:

> Most of the tribes in the interior do not grow corn but live on milk and meat, and wear skins. All the Britons dye their bodies with woad, which produces a blue colour, and shave the whole of their bodies except the head and the upper lip. Wives are shared between groups of ten or twelve men, especially between brothers and between fathers and sons; but the offspring of these unions are counted as the children of the man with whom a particular woman cohabited first.[81]

Caesar's assessment of the Germans was equally pejorative in its description of their clothing and bathing practices. "They attempt no concealment, however, of the facts of sex: men and women bathe together in the rivers, and they wear nothing but hides or short garments of hairy skin, which leave most of the body bare."[82] Given the fact that Afrocentrists and other black nationalists have conceived of themselves as radical contestors of American and European hegemony, one would think they could sympathize with the Britons and Gauls. Ancient Rome (both the Republic and the Empire) was an imperialist power that attempted to transform the indigenous culture of the people it conquered. By wearing skins, or daubing their bodies with woad, the Britons and Gauls were resisting the cultural imperialism of Rome. In short, the Britons and Gauls were claiming for themselves the right the Afrocentrists want black Americans to exercise, that is, cultural autonomy. The Afrocentrist inability to problematize Europe and see it in anything other than essentialist terms derives from a binary opposition based on the rather simplistic notion that Africa was good and Europe bad. But to construct Europe in this fashion is, as we saw in the preceding chapter, to ignore the fact that what we call Europe today has changed through and over time. What has been called "Europe" or "European" has been contested transhistorically.

Despite its hostility to all things European, Afrocentrism has not been above appropriating for itself one of the great tragedies of European history, the Holocaust. To use the word "holocaust" to describe the slave trade/slavery, as some black and Afrocentrist literature does, is nothing more than an egregious exercise in victim envy.[83] The Holocaust and the slave trade/slavery occupy separate analytical spaces. They cannot be conflated, as the Maulana Karenga does when he writes that "the severity of the violence undermines the use of the category trade as we usually think of it. What we will describe here is a Holocaust. And a Holocaust is an act of genocide so morally monstrous it is not only a crime against a people themselves but also against humanity."[84] By this definition, any severe act of violence against a people can be labeled a holocaust. The Highland Scots can claim the Clearances and their aftermath was a holocaust, the Kuwaitis could characterize Iraq's invasion of their country a holocaust, and Argentina might define the Falklands War as a holocaust. But the word cannot be used loosely to describe any and every large-scale act of inhumanity. Deborah E. Lipstadt, a Holocaust scholar, has defined the Holocaust as "unique for two primary reasons." She writes, "It was the only time in recorded history that a state tried to destroy an entire people regardless of an individual's age, sex, location, profession or belief. And it is the only instance in which the perpetrators conducted this genocide for no ostensible territorial or political gain."[85] Lipstadt's definition creates a valid and meaningful distinction between the Nazi Holocaust and every other large-scale atrocity, including the slave trade/slavery.

During the Holocaust, a form of industrial extermination, the Jewish body had no value.[86] If Jews were delivered to the camps dead, the Germans did not lose money. Indeed, the Nazis actively sought to kill the Jews, a people they demonized as the epitome of evil. Slaves, by contrast, were commodities. Despite Karenga's aversion to the word "trade," these Africans were items of consumption. They were captured, enslaved, and purchased to produce crops. They served as a substitute for other forms of labor and for modern agricultural technology. Although many died en route to market or died prematurely as a consequence of their enslavement, neither the Middle Passage, the slave trade, nor slavery itself had the goal of destroying the slaves. On the contrary, slaves were valuable and could even be insured. This can be seen, for example, in the history of the slave ship *Zong*, which "sailed from Africa to the Caribbean in 1781 loaded with 470 slaves bound for Jamaica." After twelve weeks at sea, the ship had lost more than sixty Africans and seventeen crew members. To preserve water and save "cargo" and to "allow the investors to claim a loss under their insurance policy, the captain threw 131 of the sickest slaves to their deaths."[87] When the underwriter refused to pay, the case was taken to court. There is no comparable case, according to Seymour Drescher, in the records of German courts dealing with the "disposal of captive Jews."[88]

The North American slave plantation, for all its horror and misery, was not a death camp. Its purpose was to produce commodities for the world market. Commenting on the distinction between the concentration camp and slavery, Wolfgang Sofsky says:

> The concentration camp was not a slave factory. Nonetheless, a comparison with the social form of slavery has heuristic value. It helps elucidate the transformation of human labor into *terror labor*. Slavery is always a social relation of domination and production. Slaves are part of the physical property of masters, working for them under coercion, and totally dependent on their personal arbitrary will. In contrast with wage labor, labor power is not a commodity; it is the human being himself or herself. The slave is a human being, but qua slave, he or she is a thing, an object like all other objects at the master's disposal. By social definition, the slave is therefore not a member of human society. Slaveholders have total power to dispose of their property as they wish. That power is unlimited in every

respect. Slaves are deprived not only of control over their labor, but also over themselves as people. Their owners can force them to work without a break, beat them, torment them, or hound them to death. Nonetheless, unlike the concentration camp, the world of slavery ultimately is not geared to terror and death, but to exploitation. The slave, especially under the conditions of commercial slavery, has a value and going market price. The master does not acquire slaves in order to kill them, but to put them to work for the master's benefit. Power remains a means of exploitation. Slavery is primarily a system of labor.[89]

Sofsky then moves on to the crucial distinction between slaves and the concentration camp inmates, a difference that is not accounted for in Afrocentric victim envy:

The personal dependence typical of slavery was lacking in the concentration camp. The prisoners were also exposed to arbitrary ill and whim, yet they...belonged to no one. They were controlled by an apparatus that had hunted them down and incarcerated them. It forced them to work, and in the final years of the war also leased their labor out to external beneficiaries. The SS did not operate as a slaveholder in the marketplace. Rather, as a formal agency, it defined the status of the prisoners by decree and violence. For that reason, the prisoners had neither a value nor a price. They were not traded as commodities or sold. What private companies were required to pay for prisoner labor was not a price, but an administrative leasing fee. The prisoners were subjected to a far more radical reification than any victim of slavery ever experienced. In terms of status, a slave is not a person but a thing. Yet as a living creature, the slave is a human being who has a certain property value. By contrast, the prisoner was actually depersonalized by humiliation and misery, stripped of humanity, transformed into an animal-like bundle of reactions, and ultimately killed. As barbaric as the owners often were in dealing with their slaves, the death of a slave was a loss. For power, however, the vegetating and death of the prisoners was a victory.[90]

Apparently being the descendant of slaves is not in and of itself horrible enough for some Negro Americans. Black Americans do not need to appropriate the Holocaust to understand their own suffering, however. The Middle Passage, slavery, and the limited freedom that came with emancipation have an autonomy of their own; American Negroes do not have to jump into the furnaces with the Jews to understand or legitimate their suffering. What black Americans ought to appreciate is the particularity or specificity of their own history. Victim envy is not a way of arriving at historical consciousness. Why then the appropriation of this term? The answer to this question has to do with the power of the word "holocaust" in contemporary American racial and cultural politics.

Blacks, gays, and Native Americans have all appropriated the word "holocaust," each group using the term to establish its victimhood.[91] Although it is true that blacks, gays, and Native Americans have all suffered, "it is not so that they all suffered in the same way."[92] Americans, however, are reluctant to distinguish between one type of suffering and another. Indeed, the concept of what constitutes suffering has become so elastic that practically everybody today is a victim and no one is an oppressor. Even some white men now claim this status. In this context Negroes use the word "holocaust," I think, to make a moral claim; that is, to legitimize their ancestors' suffering in a country that has not really confronted either the horrors of American Negro slavery or the central role black bondage played in the development of the United States.[93] To do so would compromise the national belief that the republic somehow exists outside of history. In the popular mind, America was and is perfect, and its history is the story of an unfolding progress. It is more comfortable to think of slavery as an aberration than to see it as a fundamental flaw in the country's institutional structure. Claiming that the Middle Passage and slavery were a holocaust is a way for Afrocentrists and other blacks to establish their people's status as victims and comment on the failure of the United States to live up to the ideas embodied in the Declaration of Independence and the Constitution.

Currently, authenticity as a victim seems to inhere in being able to lay claim to a major catastrophe that can be construed as being in some way comparable to Jewish suffering during World War II. This, I think, is because the Holocaust conferred on the Jews of Europe and their descendants a moral claim on the world's sympathy. This is what black Americans would like to have today. In fact, the quest for what John Murray Cuddihy calls the *"privilegium odiosum* of Victim"[94] has led some Afrocentrists into the distasteful practice of what Harold Brackman calls "competitive victimization." The Afrocentrist message seems to be in some cases that Jewish suffering at the hands of the Nazis pales when compared with blacks' suffering from the slave trade and slavery. Along with these assertions that "we've suffered more than you have" have also come some far-fetched claims by Afrocentrists about the dominant role of Jews in the Atlantic slave trade.

The charge that "rich Jews" played a major role in the slave trade was first made by Professor Leonard Jeffries in a July 1991 speech he gave at the Empire State Black Arts and Cultural Festival.[95] Jeffries "claimed that the 'Jewish grandees' of Spain had helped lay the foundation for the African slave trade."[96] Jewish merchants played a role in the slave trade, but their participation was not determinative, as Jeffries and some of his peers would like to think. Indeed, before Jews became involved in the African slave trade, Muslims dominated the business, a fact that seems to escape some Afrocentric commentators and complicates the discourse for those Afrocentrists and other black Americans who also happen to be Muslim. In commenting on the role of Jews in the slave trade, the Afrocentric hierophant John Henrik Clarke has stated, "We are not saying that the role of the Jews in the slave trade was any different than any other Europeans, but that it was basically the same. When they saw the opportunity to make money in the slave trade, they took advantage of this opportunity the same as other Europeans in the same business."[97] What Clarke says here is true, but to focus on the Jews to the virtual exclusion of Christian and Muslim slavers from Europe, North Africa, and the Middle East, as Jeffries and his adherents do, is clearly anti-Semitic.[98] It is also myopic to exclude the West Africans. There could not have been a slave trade without the active participation of West African elites and their surrogates. These people played a central role in the capture and sale of Africans deemed to be outsiders and therefore liable to be sold to the Europeans.[99]

Clarke's efforts to exempt himself from the charge of anti-Semitism become grotesque in the following passage from the same work quoted above: "There is a world-wide Black-White conflict which is part of the broader conflict between European and non-European people. African people are on one side of that conflict, and the people we refer to as Jews are on the other side. When I use the words Jew or Jewish people, I am referring to White people of European descent, whose culture, development and political loyalty is European. This political loyalty to Europe and the part that Jewish people still play in maintaining European world-wide power, and not anti-Semitism, is the basis of the conflict between us."[100] Even though Clarke attempts to place his critique in the context of some worldwide conflict between Europeans and blacks, what he describes is the transhistoric Jew of the anti-Semitic imagination, which is expanded to embody all the evil qualities of whiteness and European identity as well as Jewishness. Are all Jews European? Are all Jews white? Are all Europeans white? Are all European white people Jewish? This is drivel.

It does, however, serve the useful purpose of illustrating the role of Jews as scapegoats in the Afrocentric worldview.[101] Anti-Semitic black people have fabricated a transhistoric relationship between Jews and blacks that embodies oppression and exploitation, an invented pattern of Jewish machinations that they trace from the fifteenth century to the present day. In a sense, the Jewish slave trader is the forerunner of the Jewish merchant in the ghetto of the 1960s.[102] Starting from a righteous and entirely justifiable sense of anger, the more extreme Afrocentrists thus go from claiming the status of fellow holocaust victims along with the Jews, to claiming the status of chief victims who have outsuffered the Jews, to identifying Jews not as victims at all but as the primary perpetrators of the African holocaust.

Alas, the Jews are not the only minority group reviled by the Afrocentrists. Homophobia also occupies a prominent place in Afrocentric demonology. Homophobia, of course, is common throughout American society. Nevertheless, because black heterosexuality has been historically defined as animalistic, deviant, and hence abnormal by white Americans, homophobic Afrocentrists and other Negro Americans approach the subject of homosexuality from a particular perspective.[103] My point here is that historically, straight black sex, like the sexuality of other racialized subjects, has been marked as deviant. Thomas Jefferson expressed this view when he wrote, "[Negroes] are more ardent after their female: but love seems with them to be more an eager desire, than a tender delicate mixture of sentiment and sensation."[104] White sex, being "vanilla" in Jefferson's world, had no negative connotations. Black sex, being "other," did. In reaction to this negative perception, black homophobes in general have found in gay people a scapegoat for their second-class citizenship in the world of heteronormativity. Homophobic Afrocentrists in particular have gone beyond even this, to reidentify black

("African") heterosexuality as the norm and homosexuality (by definition, white) as the deviation. According to Leonard Jeffries, "The whole concept of homosexuality comes out of the caves that came out of Europe....That system is based on the male principle, men loving men as fighting men. That's the Vallhalla. That's the Nazi. That's the Greek. That's the Roman legion. That's the Catholic Church. That's not the value system Africans gave to the world, which is the duality of male and female."[105] Jeffries's hostility and his ignorance of the history of sexuality is shared by Molefi K. Asante: "The rise of homosexuality in the African-American male's psyche is real and complicated. An Afrocentric perspective recognizes its existence but homosexuality cannot be condoned or accepted as good for the national development of a strong people. It can be and must be tolerated until such time as our families and schools are engaged in Afrocentric instructions for males. The time has come for us to redeem our manhood through planned Afrocentric action. All brothers who are homosexuals should know that they too can become committed to the collective will. It means the submergence of their own wills into the collective will of our people."[106]

Both quoted passages could have been written during the Hitlerian regime or by contemporary right-wing Christians. The first incorporates the technique of the "big lie" (i.e., homosexuality is European/white and not African). Jeffries is not alone in disseminating this type of misinformation. Franz Fanon, in a flight of homophobic fancy, could write that "homosexuality is an attribute of the white race, Western Civilization."[107] The second involves an idea of community control of sexuality that is perfectly compatible with the sexual ideologies of Fascist Italy and Nazi Germany.[108] Underlying both Asante's and Jeffries's assertions about sexuality is the dubious idea that sexual practice is somehow instinctual or biological.

Recent studies in the history of sexuality and sexual preference suggest otherwise. Historian Eve Levin has written that "the psychological and medical sciences have not yet achieved a verdict on the extent to which sexuality is inherent in human biology. Certainly anatomical distinctions are generic, but the vast variation among individuals in sexual desires and sexual behavior indicates that very little in sexual behavior is instinctive."[109] Sexuality is a socially constructed activity, like other aspects of life such as the family, childhood, and recreation. Thus, when Afrocentrists such as Jeffries say there was no homosexuality in Africa, they are nominally correct, although profoundly wrong. What we call "homosexuality" in the modern world is a product of the nineteenth century.

The term "homosexual," coined in 1869 by the Swiss doctor Karoly M. Benkert, did not become a commonly used word in English until the 1890s. Same-sex behavior was also often referred to as "inversion." Of this latter term, Jeffrey Weeks has written that it "did not become common until the same period, it is only then that we find the gradual use of terms for the homosexual person which have in the twentieth century become general: words such as 'invert' and 'homosexual.' The shift in consciousness and awareness indicated by the general adoption in the contemporary homosexual world of the 'gay' (which in the last century referred to 'loose women') parallels what occurred in the late nineteenth century in the use of these new words. They are not just new labels for old realities: they point to a changing reality, both in ways a hostile society labeled homosexuality, and in the way those stigmatized saw themselves."[110] This passage points to a historical specificity about homosexuality absent in Afrocentric diatribes.

Homosexuality, like heterosexuality, is not to be understood outside of history. Neither form of sexual preference is a biological datum. Both are socially constructed identities. In the case of homosexuality, as Weeks notes, "we have to distinguish between homosexual behavior, which is universal, and a homosexual identity which is historically specific."[111] What does this mean for Africa?

It suggests that there was homosexual behavior but no homosexual consciousness before the twentieth century in Africa. In their effort to exclude Africa from a worldwide social practice, the Afrocentrists have ignored the fact that behavior often precedes consciousness.[112] What we call homosexuality today was not something introduced into the continent of Africa by Europeans, despite the silence of sources from an earlier period. The work of Edward Evans-Pritchard and others who write about sex in Africa suggests that its sexual practices were and are far more complex than American black nationalists assert. In fact, it is probably better when talking about same-sex love in Africa to speak in the plural, that is, of "homosexualities."[113] Deeply embedded in the Afrocentrists' denial of African homosexualities is both ignorance and a naive assertion of racial authenticity.

The naivete centers around the fact that cultures often have "covert categories," practices that are not explicit. People often engage privately in behaviors that are not discussed or engaged in publicly. In the case of precolonial sub-Saharan Africa, the absence of an overt homosexual culture does not mean there was no same-sex activity taking place there. In the same way that interracial sex in the United States before the 1960s was a closeted aspect of heteronormativity, homosexualities long existed, undiscussed, in black Africa and the Muslim world.[114] Afrocentric scholars are blind to this fact because of the narrow scope of sources their scholarship relies on to interpret African sexualities.

But there is another problem with the Afrocentists' claim that there were no homosexuals in Africa: this is a European argument. According to Murray and Roscoe, it was Edward Gibbon's *History of the Decline and Fall of the Roman Empire* that first argued this point of view. When the first section of the book was published in 1776, *few* white men had reached the West African interior. The first white man to do so was Mungo Park in 1789. But, secure in his ignorance of African sexual practice, Gibbon wrote, "I believe and hope, that the negroes, in their own country, were exempt from this moral pestilence [i.e., homosexual 'vice']."[115] Sir Richard Burton also shared this assumption. Writing in the nineteenth century, he observed homosexuals in the Near East and South Asia. Burton reported that "the negro race is mostly untainted by sodomy and tribalism."[116] Underlying this ignorance was the belief that "primitive" or "natural" people were free of the vice that dared not speak its name. "Since primitive man was supposed to be close to nature, ruled by instinct, and culturally unsophisticated, he had to be heterosexual, his sexual energies and outlets devoted exclusively to their 'natural' purpose: biological reproduction." In the eighteenth and nineteenth centuries, since black Africans were thought to be the most "primitive people in all humanity—if they were indeed human, which some debated," they therefore had to be the most heterosexual.[117] Thus, upon close examination, Afrocentric discourse about homosexuality is nothing more than a recycling of European ignorance and prejudice.

When the Afrocentrists and other black homophobes claim there was no homosexuality in Africa, they are establishing another test or boundary for blackness, part of a long quest for racial authenticity that began in the eighteenth century with the marginalization of racial hybrids. In Euro-American racial thought, mulattoes were dangerous and racially unstable. Historically, light-skinned blacks have also been thought of as less black because their skin does not contain the requisite amount of melanin to mark them as being purely negroid. For a time they were also believed to be incapable of reproducing themselves, as their name—which is derived from "mule"—suggests.[118] Homosexuality, being a white "thang," is alien and thus unblack. Moreover, homosexuals do not reproduce themselves. In other words, homosexuals and lesbians are not authentically black because they have betrayed the race, both by adopting a white vice and by not engaging in procreative sex. Sexuality thus operates in the same way that color historically has—as a marker of blackness within Negro America. In both cases a test of authenticity has been established to demarcate the real black from the unreal.

This attitude has created some bizarre alliances between homophobic blacks and homophobic white racists. For example, in Florida the black preacher Reverend James Sykes, a former car salesman, was quoted as saying he "would march with the Ku Klux Klan if the group held a rally against the gays only....I know they hate blacks and Jews, but I would be there with them if I knew the Klan was having a peaceful march just against the gays. For all the bad the Klan does, they are right about the gays."[119]

Comments by black homophobes, whether expressed by Asante, Jeffries, Reverend Sykes, Sister Souljah, or Green Bay Packers football star Reggie White, reflect a totalitarian view of community and sexuality in which homosexuals are viewed as a threat. According to Sister Souljah, her lesbian friend Mona wasn't "interested in viewing herself as part of a larger struggle or larger community of African people. Her entire focus was on self and pleasure."[120] Since all sexuality involves both self and pleasure, just what is at stake here is not clear. Mona and other gay black people, it would appear, have violated a community norm and consequently erased their blackness. In making the "personal political," black homophobes only recapitulate the project of the white right, whose focus on the personal has distracted the white populace of the United States for the past three decades. At a time when black people need decent housing, jobs, and schooling, obsessing about people's bed partners is both ridiculous and counterproductive. Instead, the Afrocentrists and other black homophobes should be concerned with the quality of leadership on both local and national levels in black America.

Commenting on the problem of contemporary black leadership, Professor Cornel West has written, "There has not been a time in the history of black people in this country when the quantity of politicians and intellectuals was so great, yet the quality of both groups has been so low."[121] When viewed from this perspective, the Afrocentrists are part of a larger complex of hustlers and rip-off artists besetting black America. This depredation takes place in both academic and political spheres of black life. One group pollutes the minds of schoolchildren and college students with nonsense, and the other seduces the community by claiming to represent its interest in the public sphere. Black America needs to seriously examine its use of the word "community." As it is currently employed, it provides a cover for a host of nefarious characters whose primary interest is self-aggrandizement. "Community is not a value free term. Communities not based on an ideal of justice are only mechanisms for social control,"[122] as Mary Gordon has written. This is the function of the word "community" as used by the Afrocentrists or by other black spokespeople. To give this idea of community a sense of historicity, the Afrocentrists, as we have seen, have created a narrative of the black past that is dubious.

Molefi K. Asante and other Afrocentric scholars are deeply indebted to Western conceptions of history in their efforts to create a usable present for black Americans. This new history is based, as I have argued, on European romantic racialism, which developed in the eighteenth century and flourished in the nineteenth century. Asante, I think, was being ironic when he wrote, "History teaches us that the farther a person is from an event, the more likely that person is to distort it."[123] This quotation summarizes the entire Afrocentric historical project because what they have done is misrepresent the past and recapitulate the Eurocentrist paradigm they claim to be overturning.

The Afrocentrists' racialized version of the ancient world and their distortion and appropriation of Africa, modern personages, and events amount to what Nietzsche once called a "disguised theology."[124] Like religion, Afrocentrism operates in the realm of faith or belief. One either accepts its preposterous claims or is anathematized. Doubters are either racist, if they are white, or inauthentically black and coopted by a world of Eurocentric madness. Within black America, Afrocentric scholars function like a clerisy, what Tom Wolfe has defined as "an intelligentsia with clerical presumptions."[125] In the case of the Afrocentrists, the source of their authority derives not from learning but from melanin, and melanin is the avenue of their access to true knowledge. Asante would challenge my assertion that color plays no role in understanding or accepting Afrocentrism. But in the contemporary United States, Afrocentrism is the exclusive property of Asante and his cohorts.

No white, Asian, or Latin scholar accepts or teaches Afrocentrism. Indeed, in the West and Southwest, regions of the United States that include large numbers of Mexican Americans, Afrocentrism poses a threat to cross-racial alliances, with its preposterous claims that Africans were in the new world before Columbus.[126] The anthropologist Bernard Montellano, writing about this, has the following to say: "Thus, the reader is left with the impression that all or most of the complex societies in the Americas were created or in some way influenced by African 'Blacks,' and that Native Americans were incapable of creating

any civilization or complex societies on their own." This perni-
cious idea has been uncritically accepted by some black under-
graduates and published as fact. In an article that appeared in the
Black Collegian in the 1980s, for example, Olmec civilization was
described as African in origin.

> The first civilization to appear in America, called the Olmec
> culture, was founded by Africans....The Olmecs spoke one of
> the Mande languages....The Olmec script had its origin in the
> Western Sahara....Olmecs also taught them how to grow
> crops, the (African) Olmecs also taught them how to make cal-
> endars and build step pyramids....The original Maya were
> probably Africans....The Aztecs, Zapotecs, Toltecs, and Maya
> usually occupied urban centers built by Africans, or Afro-
> Indians. Once the Indians were bound to African colonists for
> trade goods which they themselves could not produce, they
> settled in the urban centers where they learned architecture,
> writing, science, and technology from African technicians. As
> a result, the technology being brought to the Amerindians was
> of African origin.[127]

The appropriate name for this fantasy is not Afrocentrism but
Afromessianism, and it is dangerous in three ways. First, as the
quotation suggests, race and identity represent the unfortunate
proposition that evidence or some sort of factual standard are no
longer requisite for historical arguments. Confederate revisionists can claim, for example, that slavery did not cause the Civil
War.[128] In the case of the Afrocentrists and Confederate revision-

ists, historical claims are made on the basis of identity or color. Second, the Afromessianic fantasy disempowers black students by isolating them in a world that never existed and making them appear stupid to their peers. Third, these idiotic statements are insulting to Native Americans and Mexicans, who not surprisingly take offense at the derogation of their history and people.[129] How would the Afrocentrists and other black people like it if Native Americans and Mexican Americans started claiming they had taught the people of Benin smelting, or that the Ashanti stool was a cast-off of the Aztecs? In asserting that the Americas were vacant space before Africans arrived, the Afrocentrists recapitulate Hegel's assertion that Africa was a void before Europe settled it. Here again, they reveal their indebtedness to Europe.

As Brent Shaw, writing in another context, has observed, "Tinkering with…the past is a disservice to the study of history and to the reform of society. The past is dead. We cannot change it. What we can change is the future; but the way to a better future requires an unsentimental and accurate understanding of what happened in the past, and why. A more civil and humane modernity will not be achieved by tendentious misreadings of antiquity."[130] In this century black Americans have experienced a great deal of heartbreak and deception wrought by leaders who do not lead and ideas that do not empower.

How are we to explain the popularity of Afrocentrism among some black Americans? I believe that the return to communityism (discussed in the introduction) has created a space for the growth of speculative and conspiratorial ideas in black America.[131] Boring from within like boll weevils, the Afrocentrists ply shoddy political, social, and intellectual nostrums that supposedly will solve black America's problems. Because no one leader or set of ideas is capable of addressing the multitudinous ills afflicting black America at present, Afrocentrism, with its emphasis on a usable past rather than a usable present, is risible. As Booker T. Washington observed many years ago, "not all knowledge is power."

NOTES

INTRODUCTION

1. While working on this project, I was told there are other varieties of
   Afrocentrism. Just what these forms of Afrocentrism are I have not been
   able to determine, even after reading Afrocentrist literature and speaking
   to college audiences across the country. For some efforts to break out of
   the Kemetic model of Afrocentrism, see the following three works:
   Makunugu M. Akinyella, "The Foundation of a Theory of Critical Afrocentricity," in *Culture and Difference: Critical Perspectives on the Bicultural
   Experience in the United States,* ed. Antonia Darder (Westport, Conn.:
   Bergin & Garvey, 1995), 21–38. This essay calls for a more critical Afrocentric methodology. The author argues that Afrocentrism can serve as a
   form of counterhegemonic criticism of the West. I disagree. I do not
   think anything calling itself "centrism" is critical. The idea that a continent as complex as Africa could be explained by the term "centrism" is
   reductive and not a very useful analytical strategy. The essay deserves to
   be read, though, because it is more thoughtful than Asante's work. A
   similar line of argument is presented in Clinton M. Jean, *Behind the
   Eurocentric Veils* (Amherst: University of Massachusetts Press, 1991),
   98–99. See also C. Tsehloane Keto, *The African Centered Perspective of
   History* (London: Research Associates/Karnak House, 1994), 70–71. This
   book attempts to critique Afrocentric dogma about Africa as the progenitor of Western culture by advancing a "pluriversal" analysis of the origins
   of civilization.

2. Molefi Kete Asante, *Kemet, Afrocentricity, and Knowledge* (Trenton, N.J.:
   Africa World Press, 1990), 6.

3. See the following works for some examples of Afrocentric history: Molefi K. Asante, *Afrocentricity* (Trenton, N.J.: Africa World Press, 1988), passim; Asante, *Classical Africa* (Maywood, N.J.: Peoples Publishing Group, 1994); Asante, *African American History: A Journey of Liberation* (Maywood, N.J.: Peoples Publishing Group, 1995); Maulana Karenga, *Introduction to Black Studies*, 2d ed. (Los Angeles: University of Sankore Press, 1993), chap. 2; and Chancellor Williams, *The Destruction of Black Civilization* (Chicago: Third World, 1987).

4. The first quote is taken from Asante, *Kemet, Afrocentricity, and Knowledge*, 6, and the second is taken from Karenga, *Introduction to Black Studies*, 69.

5. Quoted in Gary B. Nash, Charlotte Crabtree, and Ross F. Dunn, *History on Trial* (New York: Knopf, 1997), 118.

6. See the discussion of this process in Asante's *Afrocentricity*, passim.

7. Ibid., 1.

8. Ibid.

9. Molefi K. Asante, *Afrocentric Idea* (Philadelphia, Temple University Press, 1987), 9.

10. Ibid.

11. Amos N. Wilson, *The Falsification of Afrikan Consciousness: Eurocentric History, Psychiatry, and the Politics of White Supremacy* (New York: Afrikan World Info Systems, 1993), 25.

12. George G. M. James, *Stolen Legacy* (1954; reprint, San Francisco: Julian Richardson Associates, 1988), 7, 153–154, 158.

13. Ibid., 7.

14. See, for example, Asante, *Kemet, Afrocentricity, and Knowledge*; *Afrocentric Idea; Classical Africa*, passim. Although he was not an Afrocentrist, Cheikh Anta Diop uses the term in *The African Origin of Civilization*, ed. and trans. Mercer Cook (Westport, Conn.: Lawrence Hill, 1974), 7. Diop spells the word Kemit. Karenga, *Introduction to Black Studies*, 85; Asa G. Hillard III, "Bringing Matt, Destroying Isfet: The African and African Diasporan Presence in the Study Of Ancient Kmt," in *Egypt: Child of Africa*, ed. Ivan Van Sertima (New Brunswick, N.J.: Transaction, 1995), 127–147; and finally see Williams, *Destruction of Black Civilization*, 19. These works all employ semantic sleight of hand, translating the word "Kemet" to mean "land of the blacks" rather than the Egyptian meaning, "black land."

15. Ian Shaw and Paul Nicholson, *British Museum Dictionary of Ancient Egypt* (Barcelona: Grafos S.A., 1995), 85.

16. Ibid., 148.

17. Martin Bernal, *Black Athena* (London: Free Association Books, 1987), 1:241–242. For criticisms of Bernal's volume, see *Arethusa,* (Fall 1989) (special issue); Jacques Berlinernblau, *Heresy in the University* (New Brunswick, N.J.: Rutgers University Press, 1999); Glen Bowersock, "Res-

cuing the Greeks," *New York Times Book Review,* February 25, 1996, 6–7; Jasper Griffin, "How Black Was Athena?" *New York Review of Books,* January 20, 1996, 67–72; Molly Myerowitz Levine, "The Uses and Abuses of Black Athena," *American Historical Review* 97, no. 2 (1992): 440–460; "The Marginalization of Martin Bernal," *Classical Philology* 93, no. 4 (1998): 345–363; Robert Pounder, "Black Athena 2: History without Rules," *American Historical Review* 97, no. 2 (1992): 461–464.

18. Bernal, *Black Athena,* 242.

19. For two contending points of view, see Mary Lefkowitz's courageous *Not Out Of Africa* (New York : A New Republic Book/Basic, 1996); and Tony Martin, *The Jewish Onslaught: Despatches from the Wellesley Battlefront* (Dover, Mass.: Majority, 1993).

20. I want to thank a former student, State Senator Gary Hart, for sending me a copy of this proposal. The quoted phrase is in a cover letter sent to Senator Hart by a staff member.

21. Wade W. Nobles and Lawford L. Goddard, "The Hawk Project: A Prototype Model of Male-Oriented Teenage Pregnancy Prevention" (San Francisco: Black Studies Department, San Francisco State University/Institute for the Advanced Study of Black Family Life & Culture, 1988), 12.

22. Ibid., 17.

23. See the articles in the *Columbus Dispatch,* June 16, 1993–July 6, 1997.I want to thank my friend Chris Hammett for sending me this story.

24. See the *Washington Post,* July 25, 1994.

25. For this point, see Christopher Lasch, "Black Power: Cultural Nationalism as Politics," in *The Agony of the American Left* (New York: Vintage, 1969), 134, 137; and David Gerber's "Politics of Limited Options: Northern Black Politics and the Problem of Change and Continuity in Race Relations Historiography," *Journal of Social History* 14 (Winter 1980): 235–265. For the Irish, see Oscar Handlin's classic study *Boston's Immigrants,* new ed. (Cambridge: Harvard University Press, 1959), 176.

26. For Oscar DePriest's political career, see Harold F. Gosnell, *Negro Politicians* (Chicago: University of Chicago Press, 1966), chap. 9. For Adam Clayton Powell Jr.'s election to Congress, see Jeffrey G. Stewart, *1001 Things Everyone Should Know about African American History* (New York: Doubleday, 1996), 144.

27. For an example of this tendency in Afrocentrism, see Molefi Kete Asante's response to the appointment of Joyce A. Joyce as chair of Temple University's African-American studies program in the *Chronicle of Higher Education,* November 28, 1997, A50. For an in-depth discussion of the problems in Temple University's African-American studies program, see the articles in the *Chronicle of Higher Education* dated November 28, 1997; April 18, 1997; November 1, 1996; October 25, 1996; and June 28, 1996.

28. Wilson J. Moses, "In Fairness to Afrocentrism," in *Alternatives to Afrocentrism*, ed. John J. Miller (New York: Center for the New American Community/Manhattan Institute, 1994), 21.

29. Molefi Kete Asante, "Some Concepts in Afrocentric Theory," 3. This is an unpublished paper sent to me by Theodore L. Cross, editor of *Black Issues In Higher Education*.

30. See the following works for the process of change in slave historiography: Sylvia R. Frey, *Water from the Rock* (Princeton: Princeton University Press, 1991); Eugene D. Genovese, *Roll Jordan Roll* (New York: Pantheon, 1972); Gwendolyn M. Hall, *Africans in Colonial Louisiana* (Baton Rouge: Louisiana State University Press, 1992); Michael A. Gomez, *Exchanging Our Country Marks* (Chapel Hill: University of North Carolina Press, 1998); Daniel C. Littlefield, *Rice and Slaves* (Baton Rouge: Louisiana State University Press, 1981); Phillip D. Morgan, *Slave Counterpoint* (Chapel Hill: University of North Carolina Press, 1998); Gerald W. Mullin, *Flight and Rebellion* (New York: Oxford University Press, 1972); Gerald W. Mullin, *Africa in America* (Urbana: University of Illinois Press, 1992); James Sidbury, *Ploughshares into Swords* (Cambridge: Cambridge University Press, 1997); Mechael Sobel, *The World They Made Together* (Princeton: Princeton University Press, 1987); Kenneth M. Stampp, *The Peculiar Institution* (New York: Knopf, 1956); John Thornton, *Africa and Africans in the Making of the Atlantic World, 1400–1860* (Cambridge: Cambridge University Press, 1992); and Peter Wood, *Black Majority* (New York: Knopf, 1974).

31. On the limits of some forms of identity politics, see Laura Lee Downs, "If 'Woman' Is Just an Empty Category, Then Why Am I Afraid to Walk Alone at Night? Identity Politics Meets the Post Modern Subject," *Comparative Studies in Society and History* 35 (1993): 414–437. The quotation is from Richard J. Evans, *In Defense of History* (London: Granta, 1997), 211. Chapter 7 of this splendid book should be read by every historian who has reservations about postmodernism.

32. Quoted in John Barker, *The Super Historians* (New York: Scribner's, 1982), 240.

33. Stephan Thernstrom and Abigail Thernstrom, *America in Black and White* (New York: Simon & Schuster, 1997); Dinesh D'Souza, *The End of Racism* (New York: Free Press, 1995). Anyone who reads D'Souza's book *The End of Racism* will see that he is hostile to black Americans and their culture. D'Souza has extended stereotypes that many people believe his Goan ancestors projected onto Hindus in India to American blacks. D'Souza's analysis of black American culture and history is racist. For example, in *The End of Racism*, D'Souza goes to great lengths to show that American slavery was not racist because both blacks and whites owned slaves. The issue in Southern slavery was not who owned a slave, but who was a slave. Only blacks could be slaves in the antebellum

South. D'Souza fails to note that a large percentage of the slaves held by black slave owners were members of their own families. These people could not free their kinsmen because Southern law forbade their emancipation, so they were forced to "own" them. For two devastating critiques of D'Souza's book, see George Frederickson, "Demonizing the American Dilemma," *New York Review of Books*, October 19, 1995, 10–16; and David Theo Goldberg, "Wedded to Dixie: Dinesh D'Souza and the New Segregationism," in *Racial Subjects: Writing on Race in America* (New York: Routledge, 1997), 175–226.

34. Asante, *Afrocentricity*, 106.

35. The quotation is from George Frederickson, *The Black Image in the White Mind* (New York: Harper & Row, 1971), 192. For a twentieth-century statement of the idea that blacks have been ruined by federal programs, see Charles Murray, *Losing Ground* (New York: Basic, 1984).

36. When placed in the context of American self-help ideologies, Afrocentrism is a form of positive thinking. See Charles S. Braden, *Spirits in Rebellion* (Dallas: Southern Methodist University Press, 1983); and Donald Meyer, *The Positive Thinkers* (New York: Pantheon, 1985).

37. Booker T. Washington, *Up from Slavery* (1901; reprint, New York: Norton, 1996).

38. On this point, see my essay "History Has Thrown the Colored Man Out," in my *Deromanticizing Black History: Critical Essays and Reappraisals* (Knoxville: University of Tennessee Press, 1991), 87–107. See also Michael Ignatieff, "The Narcissism of Minor Differences," in *The Warrior's Honor* (New York: Metropolitan/Holt, 1997), 62. Ignatieff makes the distinction between cultural and political belonging in this excellent book on nationalism.

39. On this point, see K. Anthony Appiah, "The Multicultural Misunderstanding," *New York Review of Books*, October 9, 1997, 30–36.

40. For the concept of "unending infallibility," see Hannah Arendt, *The Origins of Totalitarianism* (Cleveland: Meridian, 1958), 348.

41. Karl Mannheim, *Ideology and Utopia* (New York: Harcourt Brace, 1985), 192. See chapter 4 for a discussion of the "utopian mentality."

42. Ibid., 194.

43. *International Herald Tribune*, June 17, 1998, 9.

44. Stephen Howe, *Afrocentrism* (New York: Verso, 1998), 5.

45. William E. Hearn, *The Aryan Household: Its Structure and Development* (London: Longmans, Green, 1879). I would like to thank one of my undergraduate students, Brian Teeter, for bringing this quotation to my attention.

46. Richard Evans, *In Defense of History* (London: Grants, 1997), 231.

47. Ibid., 219.

48. Ibid., 124.

49. For Holocaust revisionism, see the following works: Deborah Lipstadt,

Denying the Holocaust (New York: Free Press, 1993); Charles S. Maier, *The Unmasterable Past* (Cambridge: Harvard University Press, 1988). On the issue of the uniqueness of the holocaust, see Alan S. Rosenbaum, ed., *Is the Holocaust Unique?* (Boulder: Westview, 1996). For Civil War revisionism, see James McPherson's splendid essay "The Heart of the Matter," *New York Review of Books*, October 23, 1997, 35–47. For an insightful analysis of Civil War reenactors, see Tony Horowitz, *Confederates in the Attic* (New York: Pantheon, 1998).

50. Hannah Arendt, *Origins of Totalitarianism*, 233.
51. See the following works for other discussions of Afrocentrism: Stephen Howe, *Afrocentrism*; Mary Lefkowitz, *Not Out of Africa*; and Wilson J. Moses, *Afrotopia* (New York: Cambridge University Press, 1998).
52. Friedrich Nietzsche, "On the Uses and Disadvantages of History for Life," in *Untimely Meditations*, trans. R. J. Hollingsdale (New York: Cambridge University Press, 1983), 72. With an introduction by J. P. Stern.
53. Toni Morrison, ed., *Race-ing Justice, En-gendering Power* (New York: Pantheon, 1992), xxx.
54. Quoted in Juan Williams, *Thurgood Marshall* (New York: Random House, 1998), 392.

PART ONE

1. Molefi Kete Asante, *Afrocentricity* (Trenton, N.J.: Africa World Press, 1988), 105.
2. Ibid., 36.
3. Fouad Ajami, "In Europe's Shadow," *New Republic,* November 21, 1994, 29.
4. Seth R. Schein, "Figuring the Classical in Western Culture" (manuscript in possession of the author, 1993).
5. Ibid., 4.
6. Sir William Smith, ed., *Latin English Dictionary* (New York: Barnes & Noble, 1960), 29. Both of V. Y. Mudimbe's books deal with the invented nature of Africa. See *The Invention of Africa* (Bloomington: Indiana University Press, 1988); and, *The Idea of Africa* (Bloomington: Indiana University Press, 1994).
7. C. Brace Loring et al., "Clines and Clusters versus 'Race': Test in Ancient Egypt and the Case of a Death on the Nile," in *Black Athena Revisited*, ed. Mary R. Lefkowitz and Guy Maclean Rogers (Chapel Hill: University of North Carolina Press, 1996), 156.
8. Molefi Kete Asante, *Classical Africa* (Maywood, N.J.: People's Publishing Group, 1994).
9. Denys Hay, *Europe: The Emergence of an Idea* (Edinburgh: Edinburgh University Press, 1967), 1.
10. Ibid., 58, 96, 117.

11. Ibid., preface, v–vi; introduction, xx.
12. Robert Bartlett, *The Making of Europe* (Princeton: Princeton University Press, 1994).
13. Gerard Delanty, *Inventing Europe: Idea, Identity, Reality* (New York: St. Martin's, 1995), 2.
14. Ibid., 3.
15. Molefi Kete Asante, *The Afrocentric Idea* (Philadelphia: Temple University Press, 1987), 9; Asante, *Afrocentricity*, 39; Asante, *Kemet, Afrocentricity, and Knowledge* (Trenton, N.J.: African World Press, 1990), 14; Cheikh Anta Diop, *The African Origin of Civilization*, ed. and trans. Mercer Cook (Westport, Conn.: Lawrence Hill, 1974), xiv; George G. M. James, *Stolen Legacy* (1954; reprint, San Francisco: Julian Richardson, 1988); Y. A. A. Ben-Jochannan, *Africa: Mother of Western Civilization* (Baltimore: Black Classics, 1998).
16. Michael Rice, *Egypt's Making: The Origins of Ancient Egypt, 5000–2000 B.C.* (London: Routledge, 1991), 8, 58.
17. Ibid., 39.
18. Quoted in Peter Burke, *The French Historical Revolution: The Annales School, 1929–1989* (Palo Alto, Calif.: Stanford University Press, 1990), 10.
19. For Prester John, see Ephraim Isaac, "Prester John," in *Dictionary of the Middle Ages*, ed. Joseph R. Strayer (New York: Scribner's, 1988), 10:118–119; Robert Silverberg, "Prester John in Ethiopia," in *The Realm of Prester John* (New York: Doubleday, 1972), chap. 5.
20. George M. Fredrickson, *Black Liberation* (New York: Oxford University Press, 1995), 61–63.
21. James T. Campbell, *Songs of Zion* (New York: Oxford University Press, 1995), 119.
22. Ibid., chap. 4. See also St. Clair Drake, *The Redemption of Africa and Black Religion* (Chicago: Third World, 1991); Martin R. Delany, *The Origin of Races and Color* (1879; reprint, Baltimore: Black Classics Press, 1991), 95.
23. Campbell, *Songs of Zion*, 119.
24. This discussion of black Freemasonry is based on the following works: Stephen Howe, *Afrocentrism* (New York: Verso, 1998), 66–72; William Grimshaw, *Official History of Freemasonry Among the Colored People in North America* (New York: Broadway, 1903); William A. Muraskin, *Middle-Class Blacks in a White Society: Prince Hall Free Masonry in America* (Berkeley: University of California Press, 1975); Charles Wesley, *Prince Hall: Life and Legacy* (Washington: United Supreme Council, 1983).
25. For the African origin of Masonry, see Martin R. Delany, *The Origins and Objects of Ancient Freemasonry; Its Introduction into the United States and Legitimacy among Colored Men; A Treatise Delivered before St. Cyprian Lodge; 13, June 24, A.D. 1853* (Xenia, Ohio: A. D. Delany, 1904). The quotation is on page 32.
26. Ibid.

27. David S. Wissen, "Herodotus and the Modern Debate over Race and Slavery," *Annals of Scholarship* 1 (Spring 1980): 36.

28. Constantin François de Chasseboeuf Volney, *The Ruins: Or a Survey of the Revolutions of Empires* (New York: William Davis, 1796); in *Early American Imprints, 1639–1800, The American Bibliography of Charles Evans*, ed. Clifford K. Saipton, card no. 31517 (Worcester, Mass.: American Antiquarian Society, 1959), 34–35.

29. Wissen, "Herodotus and the Modern Debate," 31.

30. Henri Grégoire, *An Enquiry Concerning the Intellectual and Moral Faculties and Literature of Negroes: Followed with an Account of the Life and Works of Fifteen Negroes and Mulattoes Distinguished in Science, Literature, and the Arts*, trans. D. B. Warden (1810; reprint, College Park, Md.: McGrath, 1967), 15, 25.

31. William Cohen, *The French Encounter with Africans: White Response to Blacks, 1530-1880* (Bloomington: Indiana University Press, 1980), 197.

32. Thomas Jefferson, *Notes on the State of Virginia* (1785; reprint, New York: Harper Torchbooks, 1964), 138.

33. Winthrop Jordan, *White over Black: American Attitudes toward the Negro, 1550–1812* (Chapel Hill: University of North Carolina Press, 1968), 429–481.

34. George Fredrickson, *White Supremacy* (New York: Oxford University Press, 1981), xi, xii.

35. Quoted in Benjamin Quarles, "Black History's Antebellum Origins," *Proceedings of the American Antiquarian Society* 89 (April 1979): 91.

36. Lydia Maria Child, *An Appeal in Favor of Americans Called Africans* (1833; reprint, New York: Arno/New York Times, 1968); Alexander Hill Everett, *America: Or a General Survey of the Political Situation of the Several Powers of the Western Continent, with Conjectures on their Future Prospects* (Philadelphia: H. C. Carey & I. Lea, 1827); Wilson Armistead, *A Tribute for the Negro* (1848; reprint, Miami: Memosyne, 1969); John Stuart Mill, "The Negro Question," quoted in Robert J. C. Young, *Colonial Desire* (London: Routledge, 1995), 128. For Herodotus, see *Herodotus: The Histories*, trans. Aubrey de Sélincourt, rev. A. R. Burn (London: Penguin, 1954), bk. 2.

37. Child, *Appeal*, 149–150.

38. Alexander Hill Everett, *America*, 214.

39. Ibid., 216.

40. Armistead, *Tribute*, 121.

41. Mill, "The Negro Question," quoted in *Colonial Desire*, 128.

42. George Wilhelm Friedrich Hegel, *The Philosophy of History* (1899; reprint, New York: Dover, 1956), 98.

43. "Uncle Tom at Home," *Putnam's Monthly* 8, no. 43 (1856): 4–5.

44. John W. Burgess, *Reconstruction and the Constitution, 1866–1876* (New York: Scribner's, 1902), 133.

45. See Clarence E. Walker, "The American Negro as Historical Outsider, 1836–1935," in *Deromanticizing Black History* (Knoxville: University of Tennessee Press, 1991).

46. Carter G. Woodson, "Negro History Week," *Journal of Negro History* 11 (April 1926): 240–244.

47. Walker, *Deromanticizing Black History*, chap. 5.

48. *In the Life: Labors of the Rt. Rev. Richard Allen* (Nashville, Tenn.: n.p., n.d.), 31–48.

49. For an outstanding discussion of the role of Haiti in the intellectual origins of Afrocentrism, see Bruce Dain's excellent article, "Haiti and Egypt in Early Black Racial Discourse," *Slavery and Abolition* 14 (December 1993): 142.

50. "The Mutability of Human Affairs," in *Classical Black Nationalism from the American Revolution to Marcus Garvey*, ed. Wilson J. Moses (New York: New York University Press, 1996), 53; see also Dain, "Haiti and Egypt," 147–149.

51. Moses, *Classical Black Nationalism*, 53, 56.

52. Ibid. See pages 54–59 for a discussion of Western empires that failed.

53. Ibid., 60–67; *David Walker's Appeal*, ed. William Loren Katz (1829; reprint, New York: Arno/New York Times, 1969).

54. Peter Hinks, *To Awaken My Afflicted Brethren: David Walker and the Problem of Antebellum Slave Resistance* (University Park: Pennsylvania State University Press, 1997).

55. *David Walker's Appeal*, 18.

56. Ibid., 29–30.

57. Robert Benjamin Lewis, *Light and Truth: Collected from the Bible and Ancient and Modern History, Containing the Universal History of the Colored and the Indian Race, from the Creation of the World to the Present Time* (1836; reprint, Portland, Me., 1844), 9–30, 192–197, 313–314, chap. 4.

58. Ibid.

59. William Wells Brown, *The Black Man: His Antecedents, His Genius, and His Achievements* (1863; reprint, New York: Thomas Hamilton, 1968), 33.

60. Ibid., 32.

61. Ibid.

62. Ibid.

63. Martin R. Delany, *The Origin of Races and Color* (1879; reprint, Baltimore: Black Classics, 1991); J. W. C. Pennington, *A Textbook of the Origins and History of the Colored People* (Hartford: L. Skinner, 1841).

64. Delany, *Origin of Races and Color*, 68.

65. Frederick Douglass, "The Claims of the Negro Ethnologically Considered," in *The Life and Writings of Frederick Douglass, 1850–1860*, ed. Phillip S. Foner (1834; New York: International, 1975), 2:301.

66. Alexander Saxton, *The Rise and Fall of the White Republic* (New York: Verso, 1990), 15.

67. George Fredrickson, *The Black Image in the White Mind* (New York: Oxford University Press, 1971), 74. See also William R. Stanton, *The Leopard's Spots: Scientific Attitudes toward Race in America, 1815-1859* (Chicago: University of Chicago Press, 1960), chap. 3. For the impact of the American School of Anthropology in England, see Young, *Colonial Desire*, chap. 5.

68. Walker, *Deromanticizing Black History*, chap. 5.

69. Edward W. Blyden, "The Negro in Ancient History," *Methodist Quarterly Review* 51 (January 1869): 81; also Delany, *Origin of Races and Color*, 45; and Brown, *Black Man*, 35.

70. Pennington, *Text Book of the Origin and History of the Colored People*, 32.

71. George Washington Williams, *A History of the Negro Race in America*, (1883; reprint, New York: Arno/New York Times, 1968), I: 24.

72. Brown, *Black Man*, 35.

73. Ibid., 36.

74. Ibid., 35–36.

75. Ibid., 34.

76. Henry Highland Garnet, "The Past and the Present Condition, and the Destiny of the Colored Race," in *Negro Social and Political Thought, 1850–1920*, ed. Howard Brotz (New York: Basic, 1966), 201.

77. *David Walker's Appeal*, 27–28. See also on this point Rev. H. Easton, "A Treatise on the Intellectual Character and Civil and Political Condition of the Colored People of the United States; and the Prejudice Exercised towards Them: With a Sermon on the Duty of the Church to Them," in *Negro Protest Pamphlets*, ed. Dorothy Porter (1837; New York: Arno/New York Times, 1969), 19.

78. *David Walker's Appeal*, 28.

79. Blyden, "The Negro in Ancient History," 83.

80. Walker, *Deromanticizing Black History*, 93.

81. Fredrickson, *The Black Image in the White Mind*, 97.

82. Ibid., chaps. 8–10. George L. Mosse, *Toward the Final Solution: A History of European Racism* (New York: Howard Fertig, 1978), 36–37. For the impact of Herder's ideas on black thinkers, see Hollis Lynch, *Edward W. Blyden* (New York: Oxford University Press, 1967), 58–65. Blyden was one of the most important black thinkers of the nineteenth century. He was not, however, a consistent thinker, as Lynch shows in his biography. In short, Blyden's ideas changed during the course of his life.

83. Quoted in Mosse, *Toward the Final Solution*, 76.

84. Lynch, *Blyden*, 54.

85. Ibid., 61.

86. Ibid., 61–62. Some of these ideas about the special nature of black people may also have come from Swedenborgianism, according to George Fredrickson; see *Black Liberation*, 61-63.

87. *California Aggie*, May 16, 1991, 1.

88. Lynch, *Blyden*, 59–62. See also Mudimbe, *The Invention of Africa* esp. 107, for a discussion of European racist thinking about Africa.

89. Lynch, *Blyden*, 59–60.

90. Edward W. Blyden, "Africa and the Africans," in *Christianity, Islam, and the Negro Race*, (1887; reprint, Edinburgh: At the University Press, 1988) 277.

91. Lynch, *Blyden*, 60. See also the letter to William Coppinger dated October 19, 1874, in *Selected Letters of Edward Wilmot Blyden,* ed. Hollis R. Lynch (Millwood: KTO Press, 1978), 173–178.

92. J. M. Ita, "Frobenius, Sénghor, and the Image of Africa," in *Modes of Thought*, ed. Robin Horton and Ruth Finnegan (London: Faber & Faber), 311. See also S. Marchand, "Leo Frobenius and the Revolt against the West" (manuscript in the author's possession).

93. Hegel, *Philosophy of History*, 99.

94. Quoted in Ita, "Frobenius, Sénghor," 307.

95. Ibid.

96. Quoted in Janet G. Vaillant, *Black, French, and African: A Life of Leopold Sedar Sénghor* (Cambridge: Harvard University Press, 1990), 124.

97. Ibid.

98. Ibid.

99. Ita, "Frobenius, Sénghor," 308.

100. Ibid., 317.

101. J. M. Ita, "Frobenius in West African History," *Journal of African History* 13, no. 4 (1972): 674.

102. Ibid.

103. Ita, "Frobenius, Sénghor," 328.

104. Ibid., 318.

105. Ibid., 325.

106. Ibid., 330.

107. Ibid.

108. Isaiah Berlin, "The Bent Twig," in *The Crooked Timber of Humanity* (New York: Knopf, 1991), 246. For a general discussion of nineteenth–century European romantic racialism, see Hans Kohn, *Prophets and Peoples* (London: Collier Macmillan, 1961), passim.

109. Berlin, *Crooked Timber*, 246.

110. Ibid.

111. Quoted in Marchand, "Leo Frobenius and the Revolt," 326.

112. Quoted in Ita, "Frobenius, Sénghor," 326.

113. Liah Greenfeld, *Nationalism* (Cambridge: Harvard University Press, 1992), 16.

114. Ibid.

115. For two insightful discussions of the contradictions in Delany's thought, see Floyd J. Miller, *The Search for a Black Nationality* (Urbana: University of Illinois Press, 1975), chaps. 3–6, 8. See also Wilson J. Moses, *The*

Golden Age of Black Nationalism, 1850–1925 (New York: Oxford University Press, 1978), chap. 1. In a superb review essay written twenty-seven years ago, Melvin Drimmer explored the conservative aims of black emigrationism: "Review Article: Black Exodus," *British Journal of American Studies* 4 (1970): 249–256.

116. Martin R. Delany, *The Condition, Elevation, Emigration, and Destiny of the Colored People of the United States* (1852; reprint, New York: Arno/New York Times, 1968), 169.

117. Drimmer, "Black Exodus," as in n. 115 passim; Moses, *Golden Age*, 68.

118. For these ideas in black thought with respect to Africa, see Moses, *Golden Age*, 20–22. For the application of the idea of racial elevation in an American context, see Clarence E. Walker, *A Rock in a Weary Land: The African Methodist Episcopal Church during the Civil War and Reconstruction* (Baton Rouge: Louisiana State University Press, 1992).

119. Alexander Crummell, "The Relations and Duties of Free Colored Men in America to Africa," in *Negro Social and Political Thought, 1850–1920*, ed. Howard Brotz (New York: Basic, 1966), 174.

120. The phrase "primitive mentality" appears in Abiola Irele, "Contemporary Thought in French-Speaking Africa," in *Africa and the West: The Legacies of Empire*, ed. Isaac James Mowe and Richard Bjornson (Westport, Conn.: Greenwood, 1986), 128.

121. Quoted in Ita, "Frobenius, Sénghor," 326.

122. Quoted in Irele, "Contemporary Thought in French-Speaking Africa," 128.

123. Ibid., 129.

124. Howe, *Afrocentrism*, chap. 14. The quotation is on page 170. For the place of Diop's scholarship in African history, see Augustin F. C. Holl, "African History: Past, Present, and Future: The Unending Quest for Alternatives," in *Making Alternative Histories*, ed. Peter R. Schmidt and Thomas C. Patterson (Santa Fe, N.M.: School of American Research Press, 1995), 197–204.

125. For some aspects of Diop's career, see Gerald Early, "Understanding Afrocentrism," *Civilization* 2 (July–August 1995): 35; Irele, "Contemporary Thought in French-Speaking Africa," 1; Diop, *African Origin*. For a black American intellectual's skepticism toward Diop's claims about Egypt, see James Baldwin, "Princes and Powers," in *Nobody Knows My Name* (New York: Dell, 1961), 46. Baldwin had the following to say about Diop: "The evening session began with a film, which I missed, and was followed by a speech from Cheikh Anta Diop, which, in sum, claimed the ancient Egyptian empire as part of the Negro past. I can only say that this question has never greatly exercised my mind, nor did M. Diop succeed in doing so—at least not in the direction he intended. He quite refused to remain within the twenty minute limit and, while his claims of the deliberate dishonesty of all Egyptian scholars may be quite well-founded for all I know, I cannot say that he convinced me. He was, however, a great success in the hall, second only, in fact, to Aimé Cesaire."

126. Irele, "Contemporary Thought in French-Speaking Africa," 132. See also Diop, *African Origin*, xiv, xvi, 2, 45, 234, 243, 244, 259.

127. Diop, *African Origin*, 234.

128. Ibid., xiv.

129. Ibid., 235.

130. Marcus Garvey, *Philosophy and Opinions of Marcus Garvey*, ed. Amy Jacques Garvey (1923; reprint, New York: Atheneum, 1969), 1:80. See also Garvey's poem "The Tragedy of White Injustice," in Marcus Garvey, *Life and Lessons*, ed. Robert Hill and Barbara Bair (Berkeley: University of California Press, 1987), 120.

131. Garvey, *Life and Lessons*, 7.

132. Ibid., 8.

133. Malcolm X, *The Autobiography of Malcolm X* (New York: Ballantine, 1973), chap. 11. See also Malcolm X, *On Afro-American History* (New York: Pathfinder, 1967), 29, 31; *Malcolm X: The Man and His Times*, ed. John Henrik Clarke (Toronto: Collier, 1969), 326–327.

134. St. Clair Drake, *Black Folk Here and There*, vol. 1 (Los Angeles: University of California–Los Angeles, 1987).

135. Howe, *Afrocentrism*, 60.

136. See, for example, the early work of Maulana Ron Karenga: "Ron Karenga and Black Cultural Nationalism," *Negro Digest* 17 (January 1968): 4–9; *The Quotable Karenga*, ed. Clyde Halisi and James Mtume (Los Angeles: US Organization, 1967). For Karenga's major statement about Afrocentrism, see *Introduction to Black Studies*, 2d ed. (Los Angeles: University of Sankore Press, 1993). Waldo Martin has written a penetrating critique of Karenga's career and ideas: "Maulana Karenga, Activist, and Intellectual; Black Cultural Nationalist (Afrocentrist)," in *Leaders From the 1960s*, ed. David De Leon (Westport, Conn.: Greenwood, 1994), 388–396. For a sampling of Afrocentric work in these fields, see the following works for psychology and biology: Daudi Ajani ya Azibo, "Advances in African Personality Theory," *Imhotep: An Afrocentric Review* 2 (January 1990); Richard King, *African Origin of Biological Psychiatry* (Germantown, Penn.: Seymour Smith, 1990); Frances Cress Welsing, *The Isis Papers* (Chicago: Third World, 1991). Afrocentric ideas about education are discussed in Haki Madhubuti and Safisha Madhubuti, *African-Centered Education* (Chicago: Third World, 1994); Mwalima J. Shujaa, *Too Much Schooling, Too Little Education: A Paradox of Black Life in White Societies* (Trenton, N.J.: Africa World Press, 1994). History is the growth industry of Afrocentric studies. See, for example, Jacob H. Carruthers, *Essays in Ancient Egyptian Studies* (Los Angeles: University of Sankore Press, 1984), 33–38; Yosef A. A. Ben-Jochannan and John Henrik Clarke, *New Dimensions in African History* (Trenton, N.J.: Africa World Press, 1991); Ivan Van Sertima, ed., *African Presence in Early Europe* (New Brunswick, N.J.: Transaction, 1988); Chancellor Williams, *The Destruction of Black Civilization* (Chicago: Third World, 1987).

137. Asante, *Kemet, Afrocentricity, and Knowledge*, 5.
138. Quoted in William Finnegan, "The Election Mandela Lost," *New York Review of Books*, October 21, 1994, 43; *New York Times*, February 7, 1997, A7.
139. K. Anthony Appiah, *In My Father's House* (New York: Oxford University Press, 1992), 26. See also Appiah's discussion of this problem in "The Conservation of 'Race,'" *Black American Literature Forum* 23 (Spring 1989): 47.
140. Edward W. Blyden, "Africa and the Africans," in *Christianity, Islam, and the Negro Race*, 272–273. See also Williams, *A History of the Negro Race in America*, 1:24.
141. Henry Louis Gates Jr., "The Weaning of America," *New Yorker*, April 19, 1993, 115.
142. Asante, *Kemet, Afrocentricity, and Knowledge*, 14.
143. Paul Gilroy, *The Black Atlantic* (Cambridge: Harvard University Press, 1993), 91.
144. Milton Meltzer, *Slavery and World History* (New York: Da Capo, 1993), 30; Barry Kemp, *Ancient Egypt* (New York: Routledge, 1991), 232. Compare the discussion of Egyptian social structure in these two texts to Molefi Kete Asante's in *Classical Africa*, 27–29.
145. Kemp, *Ancient Egypt*, 111.
146. Meltzer, *Slavery and World History*, 29–30. For an informed discussion of the lives and beliefs of ancient Egyptian workmen, see *Pharaoh's Workers*, ed. Leonard H. Lesko (Ithaca: Cornell University Press, 1994).
147. Quoted in Kemp, *Ancient Egypt*, 129.
148. Asante, *Classical Africa*, 27.
149. Ibid., 28.
150. For the concept of caste, see two older but still valuable works: Oliver Cox, *Caste, Class, and Race* (New York: Monthly Review Press, 1969), chaps. 1–7; John Dollard, *Caste and Class in a Southern Town*, 3d ed. (New York: Doubleday, 1957). I would also like to thank my colleague Barbara Metcalf for explaining the intricacies of the Indian caste system to me.
151. Asante, *Classical Africa*, 29.
152. Ibid. See also the observations about Egyptian social mobility in Rosalind M. Janssen and Jac J. Janssen, *Growing Up in Ancient Egypt* (London: Rubicon, 1990), 103.
153. Diop, *African Origin*, 205.
154. Ibid.
155. Frank J. Yurco, "Were the Ancient Egyptians Black or White?" *Biblical Archaeology Review* 15 (September–October 1989): 24. See also Brace et al., "Clines and Clusters versus 'Race,'" passim.
156. Yurco, "Were the Ancient Egyptians Black?" 24.
157. Ibid.
158. Ibid., 27. See also Meltzer, *Slavery and World History*, 30; and William Y. Adams, *Nubia: Corridor to Africa* (Princeton: Princeton University Press, 1977), chap. 2.

159. Adams, *Nubia,* 163.
160. James H. Breasted, *Ancient Records of Egypt II* (New York: Russell & Russell, 1962), 71. Breasted uses the word "Negro" in his translation instead of the word used by Egyptians to designate black people.
161. Ibid., 81. Although the quote may not be indicative of general Egyptian attitudes, it clearly indicates a significant level of animosity.
162. Adams, *Nubia,* 165.
163. Nicolas Grimal, *A History of Ancient Egypt* (London: Blackwell, 1993), 394; Yurco, "Were the Ancient Egyptians Black?" 27.
164 Williams, *A History of the Negro Race in America,* 1:17.
165. For some interesting discussions of race in the ancient world, see Frank M. Snowden Jr., *Blacks in Antiquity: Before Color Prejudice* (Cambridge: Harvard University Press, 1983). For a critique of Snowden's work, see Lloyd A. Thompson, *Romans and Blacks* (Norman and London: University of Oklahoma Press, 1989). See also the very thoughtful chapter 1 in Ivan Hannaford, *Race: The History of an Idea in the West* (Washington, D.C.: Woodrow Wilson Center Press, 1996). For race in America, see the discussion in Audrey Smedley, *Race in North America* (Boulder: Westview, 1993).
166 Asante, *Kemet, Afrocentricity, and Knowledge,* 15. See also the other texts cited in note 9, above.
167. Quoted in Chris Prouty, *Empress Taytu and Menilek II Ethiopia, 1883-1910* (New Jersey: Red Sea, 1986), 270. See also page 50.
168. James Wendy, "Perceptions from an African Slaving Frontier," *Slavery and Other Forms of Unfree Labour,* ed. Leoric Archer (London: Routledge, 1988), 130.
169. Kathryn A. Bard, "Ancient Egyptians and the Issue of Race," in *Black Athena Revisited,* ed. Mary R. Lefkowitz and Guy MacLean Rogers (Chapel Hill: University of North Carolina Press, 1996), 104.
170. Frank M. Snowden Jr., *Blacks in Antiquity,* 7. For a more sophisticated discussion of race in the ancient world, see Hannaford, *Race,* chap. 2. Hannaford should be read in conjunction with Lloyd A. Thompson, *Romans and Blacks.* This book is a very insightful and learned critique of Snowden. See especially chapters 2–3.
171. Williams, *History of the Negro Race in America,* 1:13, 15. See also Blyden, "The Negro in Ancient History," 75.
172. Petronius, *Satyricon,* trans. Michael Heseltine and W. H. D. Rouse (Cambridge: Harvard University Press, 1969), 245–247.
173. Thompson, *Romans and Blacks,* 58–59.
174. Ibid., 72.
175. Ibid., 71.
176. For this problem in the Americas, see the following works: Verena Martinez Alier, *Marriage, Class, and Colour in Nineteenth-Century Cuba* (Ann Arbor: University of Michigan Press, 1989); Carl Degler, *Neither Black Nor White* (New York: Collier Macmillan, 1971); Jay Kinsbrunner, *Not of*

Pure Blood (Durham, N.C.: Duke University Press, 1993); Peter Wade, *Blackness and Race Mixture: The Dynamics of Racial Identity in Colombia* (Baltimore: Johns Hopkins University Press, 1993); Joel Williamson, *New People* (New York: Free Press, 1980). See also Frances Gouda, *Dutch Culture Overseas* (Amsterdam: Amsterdam University Press, 1995), chap. 5. This chapter contains an interesting and insightful discussion of gender, race, and sexuality in the Dutch Indies that should be compared with the experience of black and white Southerners in the nineteenth century.

177. Ahmed Batrawi, "The Racial History of Egypt and Nubia," *Journal of the Royal Anthropological Institute of Great Britain and Ireland*, 76 (1946): 131.

178. Asante, *Classical Africa*, 43. See also the artifacts used by Diop in *African Origin of Civilization* to prove that the ancient Egyptians were black. See pp. 28–43.

179. Bard, "Ancient Egyptians and the Issue of Race," 106.

180. Ibid.

181. Asante, *Classical Africa*, 43.

182. Blyden, "The Negro in Ancient History," 84.

183. Kemp, *Ancient Egypt*, 21, 57, 59, 228. Monarchy is a constructed institution; for some interesting discussions of this process, see Peter Burke, *The Fabrication of Louis XIV* (New Haven: Yale University Press, 1992); David Cannadine, "The Context, Performance, and Meaning of Ritual: The British Monarchy and the 'Invention of Tradition,'" in *The Invention of Tradition*, ed. Eric Hobsbawm and Terrence Ranger (Cambridge: Cambridge University Press, 1983), 101–64; Linda Colley, *Britons Forging the Nation, 1707–1837* (New Haven: Yale University Press, 1992), chap. 5; T. Fujitani, *Splendid Monarchy: Power and Pageantry in Modern Japan* (Berkeley: University of California Press, 1996); Arno J. Mayer, *The Persistence of the Old Regime* (New York: Pantheon, 1981).

184. Bard, "Ancient Egyptians and the Issue of Race," 106; Yurco, "Were the Ancient Egyptians Black?" 29, 58.

185. Bard, "Ancient Egyptians and the Issue of Race," 107.

186. Ibid.

187. Cheikh Anta Diop, *Civilization or Barbarism* (Westport: Lawrence Hill, 1991), 65–67.

188. Bob Brier, *Egyptian Mummies: Unraveling the Secrets of an Ancient Art* (New York: Morrow, 1994), 201. See this book for a detailed discussion of the special problems these scientists faced in trying to restore this particular mummy. See also Nicolas Grimal, *A History of Ancient Egypt*, trans. Ian Shaw (Cambridge, Mass.: Blackwell, 1992), chap. 5, for a discussion of the changing nature of Egyptian funerary ideas. The issue of Ramses II's race is discussed in *Jet*, April 10, 1989. In this article, the Egyptian cultural emissary is quoted as saying, "We are not in any way related to the original Black Africans of the Deep South. Egypt, of course, is a country in Africa, but this doesn't mean it belongs to Africa at large. This is an Egyptian heritage, not an African heritage" (p. 25). The issue

of Ramses II's race is also discussed in Brace et al., "Clines and Clusters versus 'Race,'" 129–164, esp. 152–162.

189. Grimal, *History of Ancient Egypt*, 394.

190. These critiques of contributionism/Afrocentrism may be found in Howard Dodson, "Needed: A New Perspective on Black History," *Humanities* 2 (February 1981): 1–2; Vincent Harding, "Beyond Chaos: Black History and the Search for the New Land," *Amistead I*, ed. John A. Williams and Charles F. Harris (New York: Vintage, 1970); "History: White, Negro, and Black," *Southern Exposure* 1 (1974): 52–62; Orlando Patterson, "Rethinking Black History," *Harvard Educational Review* 41 (August 1971): 297–315; Walker, *Deromanticizing Black History*, introduction and chapter 5.

191. *Jet*, March 7, 1994, 47.

192. Peter Brown, *Augustine of Hippo* (Berkeley: University of California Press, 1969), 22, 32; W. H. C. Freud, "A Note on the Berber Background in the Life of Augustine," *Journal of Theological Studies* 43 (July–October 1941): 171–72. On Hannibal's racial origins, see the letter by Professor Sidney Halpern, Temple University, *New York Times*, July 20, 1991, 18. For a discussion of the Roman emperor Septimius Severus, also claimed as black by modern Afrocentrists, see Anthony B. Birley, *The African Emperor Septimius Severus* (London: Botsford, 1972). The word "African" in the title of the book refers to place of birth, not race or racial origin. The claim that Septimius Severus was a black African is made by Ben-Jochannan in *Africa: Mother of Western Civilization*, 159.

193. For Asante's response to Mary Lefkowitz's book *Not Out of Africa* (New York: A New Republic Book, 1996), see Molefi Kete Asante, "Reading Race in Antiquity: The Many Fallacies of Mary Lefkowitz," personal e-mail, February 19, 1996. For Cleopatra's family history, see Walter M. Ellis, *Ptolemy of Egypt* (New York: Routledge, 1994); Michael Grant, *Cleopatra* (New York: Barnes & Noble, 1992), 3, 42; John Whitehorn, *Cleopatras* (New York: Routledge, 1994).

194. Asante, "Reading Race in Antiquity," 5. See also the response of Charles S. Finch III, "Still Out of Africa," to Lefkowitz's book. This is another Afrocentric exercise in character assassination masquerading as scholarship. This article was sent to me by a friend and is undated.

195. Ben-Jochannan, *Africa: Mother of Western Civilization*, 112.

196. John Henrik Clarke, "African Warrior Queens," in *Black Women in Antiquity*, ed. Ivan Van Sertima (New Brunswick, N.J.: Transaction, 1988), 28. Compare the essays in the Van Sertima volume to Gay Robbins, *Women in Ancient Egypt* (Cambridge: Harvard University Press, 1993). Robbins's book is a historically grounded study of women in the ancient world. The essays in Van Sertima are pure fantasy. See Chancellor Williams, *The Destruction Of Black Civilization*, pp. 71–87, for a discussion of the mulatto problem in Egyptian history.

197. Grant, *Cleopatra*, xi. See also on this point Lucy Hughes-Hallett, *Cleopa-*

tra (New York: HarperCollins, 1990), 14–15; and Mary Hamer, *Signs of Cleopatra* (London: Routledge, 1993), 5.

198. Grant, *Cleopatra*, 42–43.

199. Ibid., 4–5; Julia Sampson, *Nefertiti and Cleopatra: Queen-Monarchs of Ancient Egypt* (London: Rubicon, 1985), 104.

200. Grant, *Cleopatra*, 5.

201. For the various meanings accorded color in the Caribbean and in North and South America, see Carl Degler, *Neither Black Nor White*; F. James Davis, *Who Is Black?* (University Park: Pennsylvania State University Press, 1991), 5; Virginia R. Dominguez, *White by Definition* (New Brunswick, N.J.: Rutgers University Press, 1986); Marvin Harris, *Patterns of Race in the Americas* (New York: Walker, 1964), 36; Jordan, *White over Black*, chap. 4; Joel Williamson, *New People*, chap. 1.

202. Quoted in Thompson, *Romans and Blacks*, 158.

203. For this point, see the items cited in note 163.

204. Malcolm X, *On Afro-American History*, 49.

205. The Jungle Brothers, "Done by the Forces of Nature," Warner Brothers Records, W2-26072, 1989.

206. Quoted in Nicholas Davis, *Queen Elizabeth II: A Woman Who Is Not Amused* (New York: Birch Lane, 1994), 453; Asante, *Afrocentricity*, 39.

207. Grant, *Cleopatra*, 26–27. See also Whitehorn, *Cleopatras*, for a discussion of royal incest in the Ptolemaic dynasty, 174, 77, 85, 90–91.

208. Whitehorn, *Cleopatras*, 175.

209. Ibid., 98, 121.

210. Grant, *Cleopatra*, 40; Ellis, *Ptolemy of Egypt*, 66.

211. Asante, *Kemet, Afrocentricity, and Knowledge*, 15.

212. Halisi and Mtume, *Quotable Karenga*, 5. "Silence" may be the wrong word here. The proper word for the Afrocentrist treatment of slavery may perhaps be "simplistic."

213. John Thornton, *Africa and Africans in the Making of the Atlantic World, 1400-1680* (Cambridge: Cambridge University Press, 1992), 74; Claude Meillassoeux, *The Anthropology of Slavery: The Womb of Iron and Gold*, trans. Alide Dasnois (Chicago: University of Chicago Press, 1990), 291.

214. Nathan Huggins, *Black Odyssey: The African American Ordeal in Slavery* (New York: Vintage, 1977), 20.

215. *California Aggie*, May 16, 1991, 1.

216. Asante, *Afrocentricity*, 66.

217. Ibid., 66.

218. *Equiano's Travels*, edited and abridged by Paul Edwards (1789; London: Heinemann Educational Books, 1967), 26.

219. Ibid., 35.

220. Ibid., 43–44.

221. Jon F. Sensbach, "A Separate Canaan: The Making of an AFRO Moravian World in North Carolina, 1763-1856" (Ph.D. diss., Duke University, 1991), 18.

222. Ibid., 18.

223. "Abou Bekir Sadiki, Alias Edward Doulan," *Journal of Negro History* 31 (1936): 53.

224. James Mellon, ed., *Bullwhip Days* (New York: Weidenfeld & Nicolson, 1981), 50.

225. Sidney W. Mintz, *Caribbean Transformations* (Baltimore: Johns Hopkins Press, 1974), 60.

226. Robin Blackburn, *The Overthrow of Colonial Slavery, 1776-1848* (New York: Verso, 1988), 20.

227. Phillip Morgan, "British Encounters with Africans and African-Americans, circa 1600–1780," in *Strangers within the Realm*, ed. Bernard Bailyn and Philip D. Morgan (Boston: Beacon, 1992), 17.

228. Sidney Mintz and Richard Price, *The Birth of African American Culture* (Boston: Beacon, 1992), 17.

229. Frederick Douglass, *My Bondage and My Freedom* (1855; reprint, New York: Arno/New York Times, 1969), 199.

230. Gerald W. Mullin, *Flight and Rebellion* (New York: Oxford University Press, 1972), 142–163.

231. John Lofton, *Insurrection in South Carolina* (Yellow Springs, Ohio: Antioch Press, 1964), 131–143.

232. Edwin S. Redkey, *A Grand Army of Black Men* (Cambridge: Cambridge University Press, 1993), 140.

233. See, for example, Gwendolyn M. Hall, *Africans in Colonial Louisiana* (Baton Rouge: Louisiana State University Press, 1992); Daniel C. Littlefield, *Rice and Slaves* (Baton Rouge: Louisiana State University Press, 1981); Gerald W. Mullin, *Flight and Rebellion*; Mechael Sobel, *The World They Made Together* (Princeton: Princeton University Press, 1987); Peter Wood, *Black Majority* (New York: Knopf, 1974).

234. Degler, *Neither Black Nor White*; Kinsbruner, *Not of Pure Blood*; Magnus Morne, *Race Mixture in the History of Latin America* (Boston: Little, Brown, 1967); Gerald M. Sider, *Lumbee Indian Histories* (New York: Cambridge University Press, 1994); Thomas Skidmore, *Black into White* (1974; reprint, Durham: Duke University Press, 1993); Wade, *Blackness and Race Mixture.*

235. Quoted in Julyan G. Peard, "The Tropicalista School of Medicine of Bahia, Brazil, 1860–1889" (Ph.D. diss., Columbia University, 1990), 198–199.

236. Peter Wade, *New York Times*, March 29, 1994, A3.

237. Henry Highland Garnet, "The Past and the Present Condition, and the Destiny of the Colored Race," in *Negro Social and Political Thought*, 199–201.

238. Mavis Campbell, *The Maroons of Jamaica, 1655-1796* (Trenton, N.J.: Africa World Press, 1990), 153–154, 228; Michael Craton, *Testing the Chains* (Ithaca: Cornell University Press, 1982), 65. Orlando Patterson, *The Sociology of Slavery* (London: Cox & Wayman, 1967), 267.

239. Craton, *Testing the Chains*, 65, 66; Campbell, *Songs of Zion*, 245; John Gabriel Steadman, *Narrative of a Five Years' Expedition against the Revolted Negroes of Surinam*, ed. Richard Price and Sally Price (1796; Baltimore: Johns Hopkins University Press, 1992), 227.

240. Craton, *Testing the Chains*, 66; Campbell, *Maroons of Jamaica*, 204.

241. Campbell, *Maroons of Jamaica*, 204.

242. Ibid., 228.

243. Quoted in Monica Schuler, *Alas, Alas, Kongo* (Baltimore: Johns Hopkins University Press, 1980), 68.

244. Campbell, *Maroons of Jamaica*, 251.

245. Ibid., 48; Craton, *Testing the Chains*, 77; Barbara K. Kopytoff, "Jamaican Maroon Political Organization: The Effect of the Treaties," *Social and Economic Studies* 25 (June 1976): 88.

246. *Equiano's Travels*, 172.

247. Jõao José Reis, *Slave Rebellion*, trans. Arthur Brakel (Baltimore: Johns Hopkins University Press, 1993), 148.

248. Ibid., 121.

249. Ibid., 122.

250. Eduardo Silva, *Prince of the People*, trans. Moyra Ashford (New York: Verso, 1993), 61–62. See also Emilia Viotti da Costa, *Crowns of Glory, Tears of Blood* (New York: Oxford University Press, 1994), 195.

251. Miguel Barnet, *Biography of a Runaway Slave*, trans. W. Nick Hill (Willimantic, Conn.: Curbstone, 1994), 37.

252. David Potter, *The Impending Crisis, 1840-1861* (New York: Harper & Row, 1976), 461.

253. Randall M. Miller, ed., *Dear Master: Letters of a Slave Family* (Ithaca: Cornell University Press, 1978), 47.

254. Ibid.

255. Ibid., 75.

256. Ibid., 101, 407. See also Bell I. Wiley, ed., *Slaves No More: Letters from Liberia, 1833–1869* (Lexington: University of Kentucky Press, 1980), 6, 28, 106, 183.

257. Walker, *Deromanticizing Black History*, 43. See also note 46.

258. Ibid., 47.

259. Campbell, *Songs of Zion*, vii.

260. Quoted in Walker, *Deromanticizing Black History*, 11.

261. Alexander Crummell, "The Destined Superiority of the Negro," in *Civilization and Black Progress: Selected Writings of Alexander Crummell on the South*, ed. J. R. Oldfield (Charlottesville: University Press of Virginia, 1995), 48.

262. Quoted in Walter Williams, *Black Americans and the Evangelization of Africa, 1877–1900* (Madison: University of Wisconsin Press, 1982), 36.

263. Quoted in Leon Litwack, *Been in the Storm So Long* (New York: Knopf, 1979), 543.

264. Ibid., 539.

265. This idea is developed in Moses, *Golden Age of Black Nationalism*, chaps. 2–3. See also Leonard I. Sweet, *Black Images of America, 1784-1870* (New York: Norton, 1976), passim.

266. *Christian Recorder*, November 21, 1868.

267. Le Roi Jones, *Home* (New York: Morrow, 1966), 111.

268. Ibid.

269. Joan W. Scott, "History in Crisis? The Other Side of the Story," *American Historical Review* 94 (June 1989): 690.

270. Asante, *Kemet, Afrocentricity, and Knowledge*, 5.

271. Asante, *Afrocentricity*, 106.

272. Karenga, "Ron Karenga and Black Cultural Nationalism," 5.

273. Asante, *Afrocentricity*, 31.

274. Ibid., 22–24.

275. Ibid., 24–30.

276. For an incisive critique and history of mind cure, see Donald Meyer, *The Positive Thinkers* (New York: Pantheon, 1980). See also Wendy Kaminer, *I'm Dysfunctional, You're Dysfunctional* (Reading, Mass.: Addison-Wesley, 1992), 5.

277. Kaminer, *I'm Dysfunctional, You're Dysfunctional*, 20.

278. See Linda Harrison, "On Cultural Nationalism," in *The Black Panthers Speak*, ed. Philip S. Foner (New York: Da Capo, 1995), 151.

279. Welsing, *Isis Papers*, chap. 1.

280. Asante, *Afrocentricity*, 81.

281. Quoted in Karen J. Winker, "Flouting Convention," *Chronicle of Higher Education*, September 28, 1994, A8.

282. Professor Mia Bay made this point in a thoughtful and provocative paper she sent me several years ago. The paper was titled "The Historical Origins of Afrocentrism." This manuscript is in my possession.

283. Frederick Douglass, "The Claims of the Negro Ethnologically Considered," in *Life and Writings of Frederick Douglass*, 2:307.

PART TWO

1. The first quote is in Theodore Rosengarten, *All God's Dangers: The Life of Nate Shaw* (New York: Vintage, 1984), 233. The second quote "Not all knowledge is power" comes from Louis Harlan, *Booker T. Washington: The Wizard of Tuskegee, 1901–1915* (New York: Oxford University Press, 1983), 1:149.

2. On this point see Manning Marable, *Black Leadership* (New York: Columbia University Press, 1998), pt. 4; Cornell West, *Race Matters* (Boston: Beacon, 1993), chap. 3.

3. As I use the term "right," I am not referring solely to Republicans but to a general shift in American racial sensibilities that includes Republicans, Democrats, whites, and blacks, all of whom seem to be hostile to govern-

ment-sponsored racial amelioration. For a thoughtful discussion of the multiple positions on race within the white right, see Howard Winnant, "Behind Blue Eyes: Whiteness and Contemporary U.S. Racial Politics," *New Left Review* 225 (September–October 1997): 73–88. See also "Excerpts from Round Table with Opponents of Racial Preference," *New York Times*, December 22, 1997, national edition, A16. This article contains a representative sample of what I call here a rightward drift on race.

4. Eric Foner, *Reconstruction: America's Unfinished Revolution, 1863–1877* (New York: Harper & Row, 1989), 248.

5. The following works contain interesting discussions of how the law functioned to establish racial inequality during Reconstruction and after. William Gillette, *Retreat from Reconstruction, 1869–1879* (Baton Rouge: Louisiana State University Press, 1979), passim; Foner, *Reconstruction*, chap. 9; John Hope Franklin, *Reconstruction after the Civil War* (Chicago: University of Chicago Press, 1966), 202, 206–209; Brook Thomas, ed., *Plessy v. Ferguson* (New York: Bedford, 1977), 1–38.

6. For the origins of Jim Crow in southern housing, see Howard Rabinowitz, *Race Relations in the Urban South* (New York: Oxford University Press, 1978). For the origins of Jim Crow, see C. Vann Woodward, *The Strange Career of Jim Crow* (New York: Oxford University Press, 1974). Glenda Gilmore's book *Gender and Jim Crow* (Chapel Hill: University of North Carolina Press, 1996) is not completely satisfying in its explanation of the role of black and white women in the origins of Jim Crow. Two excellent books on race and suffrage are William Gillette, *The Right to Vote: Politics and the Passage of the Fifteenth Amendment* (Baltimore: Johns Hopkins University Press, 1965); and Morgan J. Kousser, *The Shaping of Southern Suffrage: Restriction and the Establishment of the One-Party South, 1880–1910* (New Haven: Yale University Press, 1974), esp. 56–57, 170–171, 202. Both of these books show the ambivalence with which the nation embraced the idea of black suffrage.

7. The following articles in *Jet* illustrate this point: July 15, 1996, 7–8; October 6, 1997, 23–24; December 15, 1997, 46–47; February 22, 1999, 38. See also "A Mounting War on Bias,"*New York Times*, January 15, 1998, A21; and for the white supremacist right, see Michael Barkan, *Religion and the Racist Right* (Chapel Hill: University of North Carolina Press, 1994); Kevin Lynn and Gary Gerhardt, *The Silent Brotherhood* (New York: Free Press, 1989); Andrew MacDonald, *The Turner Diaries* (New York: Barricade, 1980); Michael Novick, *White Lies, White Power* (Monroe, Me.: Common Courage, 1990).

8. On this point, see "Clinton Debates 9 Conservatives on Racial Issues," *New York Times*, December 20, 1997. The *New York Times* and other journals of public opinion always refer to the critics of affirmative action as conservative. This label is a misnomer, since these critics are really reacting to public policy, not conserving it. In the debate about affirmative action, President Clinton is the conservative; his critics are reactionaries.

See also *New York Times,* December 18, 1997, A21, for another example of conservative voices in the debate about race (affirmative action). Finally, see "Blacks Recruited by 'Right' to End Preference," *New York Times,* December 17, 1997, A12.

9. For a superb discussion of the limits of color-blindness, see Amy Gutman's essay "Responding to Racial Injustice," in *Color Conscious,* ed. K. Anthony Appiah and Amy Gutman (Princeton: Princeton University Press, 1996), 106–178. See also Glenn C. Loury, "Color-Blinded," *New Republic,* August 17–24, 1998, 12.

10. Patricia Williams, *Seeing a Color-Blind Future* (New York: Noonday, 1997), 4.

11. *New York Times,* September 26, 1999, 4.

12. For whiteness studies, see the following works: Maurice Berger, *White Lies* (New York: Farrar Straus Giroux, 1999); Ruth Frankenberg, ed., *Displacing Whiteness: Critical Essays in Social and Cultural Studies* (Durham, N.C.: Duke University Press, 1997). The introduction to this book gives good insight on the unmarked nature of whiteness. See also Frankenberg's *White Women, Race Matters: The Social Construction of Whiteness* (Minneapolis: University of Minnesota Press, 1993). For the historical construction of whiteness, see Karen Brodkin, *How Jews Became White Folks* (New Brunswick, N.J.: Rutgers University Press, 1998); Noel Ignatiev, *How the Irish Became White* (New York: Routledge, 1995); Matthew Frye Jacobson, *Whiteness of a Different Color* (Cambridge: Harvard University Press, 1998); George Lipsitz, *The Possessive Investment in Whiteness* (Philadelphia: Temple University Press, 1998); David Roediger, *The Wages of Whiteness: Race and the Making of the American Working Class* (New York: Verso, 1991).

13 Frankenberg, *Displacing Whiteness,* 1.

14. Quoted in W. E. B. Du Bois, *Black Reconstruction* (New York: Russell & Russell, 1935), 276.

15. Quoted in David W. Bowen, *Andrew Johnson and the Negro* (Knoxville: University of Tennessee Press, 1989), 137.

16. Quoted in Richard Hofestadter, *The American Political Tradition and the Men Who Made It* (New York: Vintage, 1989), 198–199.

17. Quoted in Foner, *Reconstruction,* 587.

18. See, for example, the discussion of free Negro life in the colonial and antebellum period in Ira Berlin, *Slaves without Masters* (New York: Pantheon, 1974); James Oliver Horton and Lois E. Horton, *In Hope of Liberty* (New York: Oxford University Press, 1997); Leon Litwack, *North of Slavery* (Chicago: University of Chicago Press); Gary Nash, *Forging Freedom* (Cambridge: Harvard University Press, 1988). For the postbellum period and the twentieth century, see William Cohen, *At Freedom's Edge* (Baton Rouge: Louisiana State University Press, 1991); Roger Lane, *Roots of Violence in Black Philadelphia, 1860–1900* (Cambridge: Harvard University Press, 1986); and Lane, *William Dorsey's Philadelphia and Ours* (New

York: Oxford University Press, 1991); Leon Litwack, *Trouble in Mind* (New York: Knopf, 1998); Thomas Philpott, *The Slum and Ghetto* (Belmont, Calif.: Wadsworth, 1991); Melvin L. Oliver and Thomas M. Shapiro, *Black Wealth, White Wealth* (New York: Routledge, 1997); Douglass C. Massey and Nancy A. Denton, *American Apartheid* (Cambridge: Harvard University Press, 1993); Thomas J. Sugrue, *The Origins of the Urban Crisis* (Princeton: Princeton University Press, 1996).

19. Quoted in "Race on Screen and Off," *The Nation*, December 29, 1997, 4.
20. For a brilliant and frightening discussion of the problem of white status anxiety, see William Finnegan's *Cold New World* (New York: Modern Library, 1999), bk. 4.
21. Bob Herbert, "The Respect Divide," *New York Times*, June 16, 1997, A15.
22. West, *Race Matters*, 38.
23. Brian Fay, *Critical Social Science* (Ithaca: Cornell University Press, 1987), 73.
24. For this point, see *Atonement: The Million Man March* (Cleveland: Pilgrim, 1996). In this book participants in the march repeatedly invoke the concept of community to explain their attendance at the event. See also Michael A. Cotman, *Million Man March* (New York: Crown Trade Paperbacks, 1995).
25. My analysis of the meaning of the Million Man March and its place in American protest may be found in the British journal *Red Pepper*, December 19, 1995, 24–25.
26. Quoted in Cha-Jua and Lang, "Providence, Patriarchy, Pathology," *New Politics* 6, no. 2 (1997): 63.
27. Paul Gilroy, *Small Acts* (London: Serpents Tail, 1993), 204.
28. Ibid. For Adolph Reed's comments about community, see Manning Marable, "Black (Community) Power!" *The Nation*, December 22, 1997, 23. For a superb analysis of Farrakhan's political and social ideology, which places him in the mainstream of right-wing American politics, see Robert Singh, *The Farrakhan Phenomenon* (Washington, D.C.: Georgetown University Press, 1997). See also Adolph Reed, "Beyond the Monolith," *Boston Sunday Globe*, July 24, 1994, 7. This article does an excellent job of showing how black America cannot be subsumed or explained by a unitary rubric.
29. Molefi Kete Asante, *Afrocentricity* (Trenton, N.J.: Africa World Press, 1988), 106.
30. Ibid., 26.
31. bell hooks, *Black Looks* (Boston: South End, 1992), 93.
32. Gerald Early, *Daughters on Family and Fatherhood* (New York: Addison-Wesley, 1994), 89–113.
33. Ibid., 100.
34. Paul M. Barrett, *The Good Black* (New York: Dutton, 1999); Ellis Close, *The Rage of a Privileged Class* (New York: HarperCollins, 1993); Gerald Early, ed., *Lure and Loathing* (New York: Allen Lane, 1992); Jake Lamar,

Bourgeois Blues (New York: Summit, 1991); Itabari Njeri, *The Last Planta-tion* (Boston: Houghton Mifflin, 1997); Jill Nelson, *Volunteer Slavery* (Chicago: Noble, 1993).

35. August Meier, *Negro Thought in America, 1880–1915* (Ann Arbor: University of Michigan Press, 1963), 24.

36. Ibid.

37. Ibid.

38. Quoted in Cha-Jua and Lang, "Providence, Patriarchy, Pathology," 63.

39. For the details of these three men's lives, see the following works: On T. Thomas Fortune, see Emma Lou Thornbrough, *T. Thomas Fortune* (Chicago: University of Chicago Press, 1972), 78. For the life of Booker T. Washington, see Harlan, *Booker T. Washington*, vols. 1–2. Williams's life and career is examined in John Hope Franklin's *George Washington Williams* (Chicago: University of Chicago Press, 1985).

40. Thornbrough, *T. Thomas Fortune*, 78.

41. George Washington Williams, *A History of the Negro Race in America, 1619–1880* (1883; New York: Putnam, 1883), 11:257–258.

42. Quoted in William Appleman Williams, *The Contours of American History* (Cleveland: World, 1961), 323.

43. *Booker T. Washington*, ed. E. L. Thornbrough (Englewood Cliffs, N.J.: Prentice-Hall, 1969), 44.

44. On the problem of capital, see David A. Gerber, "Politics of Limited Options: Northern Black Politics and the Problem of Change and Continuity in Race Relations Historiography," *Journal of Social History* 14 (Winter 1980): 235–265.

45. I made this point in my essay "How Many Niggers Did Karl Marx Know?" in my *Deromanticizing Black History: Critical Essays and Reappraisals*, by Clarence E. Walker (Knoxville: University of Tennessee Press, 1991), 30–33.

46. See, for example, the following works for examples of the discrimination and terrorization of emancipated populations described in the text: Christopher Fyfe, *Africanis Horton, 1835–1883* (New York: Oxford University Press, 1972); Pierre Birnbaum and Ira Katznelson, eds., *Paths of Emancipation: Jews, States, and Citizenship* (Princeton: Princeton University Press, 1995); Leon Litwack, *Trouble in Mind* (New York: Knopf, 1998); and Leo Spitzer, *Lives in Between: Assimilation and Marginality in Austria, Brazil, and West Africa* (London: Cambridge University Press, 1989).

47. For the use of the term "enslavement," see Molefi K. Asante and Mark T. Mattson, *The African-American Atlas* (New York: Macmillan, 1998), chaps. 3–4.

48. James Horton, "Making Slavery Palatable to the Bermuda-shorts Set," *New Yorker*, June 14, 1999, 29–30.

49. See Colin Palmer's effort to bring some analytical precision to the use of the word "diaspora" in his essay "Defining and Studying the Modern

African Diaspora," *Perspectives* 36 (September 1998): 1, 22–25. Palmer also fails to take note of the fact that Africans were commodities. In short, they were not agents of their history.

50. For a valuable discussion of the concept of diaspora, see "Diaspora and Immigration," *South Atlantic Quarterly* 98 (Winter-Spring: 1999) (special issue, ed. V. Y. Mudimbe with Sabine Engle). As used in contemporary discourse, the term "diaspora" operates as a portmanteau word. That is, every historical experience in this country can be packed in the case. What special claim, then, are black people making about their history when they use this word?

51. Quoted in Meier, *Negro Thought*, 53.

52. Ibid.

53. Carter G. Woodson, "Negro Life and History in Our Schools," *Journal of Negro History*, July 4, 1979, 274–275. See Dickson D. Bruce, "Ancient Africa and the Early Black American Historians, 1883–1915," *American Quarterly* 36 (Winter 1984): 683–699.

54. These books illustrate my point: for Germany, see Saul Friedländer, *Nazi Germany and the Jews: The Years of Persecution, 1933–1939* (New York: HarperCollins, 1997); Wolfgang Sofsky, *The Order of Terror: The Concentration Camp*, trans. William Templer (Princeton: Princeton University Press, 1997). For Japan, see Ines Chang, *The Rape of Nanking* (New York: Basic, 1997); George Hicks, *The Comfort Women* (New York: Norton, 1994). For Yugoslavia, see Denis Del Favero, *Motel Vilina Vlat* (Sydney: Websdale, 1995).

55. See, for example, John Henrik Clarke, *African People in World History* (Baltimore: Black Classic, 1978); Yosef A.A. Ben-Jochannan and John Henrik Clarke, *New Dimensions in African History* (Trenton, N.J.: Africa World Press, 1991); Yosef A.A. Ben-Jochannan, *Africa: Mother of Western Civilization* (Baltimore: Black Classic, 1988); *Black Man of the Nile and His Family* (Baltimore: Black Classic, 1989); Ivan Van Sertima, ed., *African Presence in Early Europe* (New Brunswick, N.J.: Transaction, 1988); Chancellor Williams, *The Destruction of Black Civilization* (Chicago: Third World, 1987).

56. Maulana Karenga, *Introduction to Black Studies*, 2d ed. (Los Angeles: University of Sankore Press, 1993), 169–170.

57. *Africa and Africans as Seen by Classical Writers: The William Leo Hansberry African History Note Book*, ed. Joseph E. Harris (Washington, D.C.: Howard University Press, 1977), xi. Hansberry was not an Afrocentrist, but his work echoes themes and ideas found in contemporary Afrocentrism.

58. John Henrik Clarke, "Historian, Educator, Author, Editor, Lecturer," in *First Word, Black Scholars, Thinkers, Warriors, Knowledge, Wisdom, Mental, Liberation*, ed. Kwaku Person-Lynn (New York: Harlem River, 1996), 13.

59. Friedrich Nietzsche, "On the Uses and Disadvantages of History for

Life," in *Untimely Meditations*, trans. R. J. Hollingdale (Cambridge: Cambridge University Press, 1991), 76. With an introduction by J. P. Stern.

60. Asante, *Afrocentricity*, 7.
61. Rosengarten, *All God's Dangers*, 543.
62. Asante, *Afrocentricity*, 7.
63. For a general discussion of Washington and his views of Africa, see Louis R. Harlan's article "Booker T. Washington and the White Man's Burden," in *Booker T. Washington in Perspective: Essays of Louis R. Harlan*, ed. Raymond W. Smock (Jackson: University Press of Mississippi, 1988), 69.
64. Ibid., 75.
65. Professor Kevin Grant, personal communication with author, February 1, 1998. Grant is professor of British Empire history at Hamilton College.
66. Person-Lynn, *First Word*, 13 (see p. 158, note 58 above).
67. *Pawnship in Africa: Debt Bondage in Historical Perspective*, ed. Toyui Falola and Paul E. Lovejoy (Boulder: Westview, 1994), 2.
68. Reverend Peter Williams, "An Oration on the Abolition of the Slave Trade; Delivered in the African Church, in the City of New York, January 1, 1808," in *Early Negro Writing 1760–1837*, selected and introduced by Dorothy Porter (1808; Baltimore: Black Classics, 1995), 347.
69. Henry Sipkins, "An Oration on the Abolition of the Slave Trade, Delivered in the African Church, in the City of New York, January 2, 1809. With an Introductory Address by Henry Johnson," in *Early Negro Writing*, 395.
70. Quoted in K. Anthony Appiah, "Europe Upsidedown," *Times Literary Supplement*, February 12, 1993, 24–25.
71. Quoted in Alexis Sinduhijie, "Welcome to America," *Transition* 8, no. 2 (1999): 16. See also the discussion of black Americans and Africa in the *New York Times*, December 27, 1999, A4.
72. Falola, *Pawnship in Africa*, 2.
73. *The Travels of Mungo Park*, ed. Ronald Miller (1798; New York: Dutton, 1960), 190.
74. E. A. Ayandele, *The Missionary Impact on Modern Nigeria, 1842–1914* (New York: Humanities, 1966), 162. A similar point about African displeasure with traditional society is made in Stephen Taylor, *Shaka's Children: A History of the Zulu People* (London: HarperCollins, 1995), 98.
75. Ayandele, *The Missionary Impact on Modern Nigeria*, 162.
76. Franz Fanon, *Black Skin White Masks* (New York: Grove, 1967), 10.
77. Ranajit Guha, *Dominance without Hegemony* (Cambridge: Harvard University Press, 1997), 11.
78. Appiah, "Europe Upsidedown," 25.
79. "The Tragedy of White Injustice," in *Marcus Garvey: Life and Lessons*, ed. Robert Hill and Barbara Bair (Berkeley: University of California Press, 1987), 120.

80. Malcolm X, *On Afro-American History* (New York: Pathfinder, 1990), 31.
81. Caesar, *The Conquest of Gaul,* trans. S. A. Handford, rev. Jane F. Gardner (London: Penguin, 1982), 111. See also Tacitus, *The Agricola and the Germania,* trans. H. Mattingly, rev. S. A. Handford (London: Penguin, 1970), 114, 140.
82. Caesar, *Conquest of Gaul,* 143.
83. See S. Enderson, *The Black Holocaust for Beginners* (New York: Writers and Readers Publishing, 1995); John Henrik Clarke, "Black Demagogues and Pseudo-Scholars," in *Black Books Bulletin: Words, Work* 16 (Winter 1993–1994): 11; Karenga, *Introduction to Black Studies,* 115–124; Tony Martin, *The Jewish Onslaught* (Dover, Mass.: Majority, 1993), 37. The fullest use of the term "African holocaust" occurs in *The Secret Relationship between Blacks and Jews,* vol. 1 (Chicago: Nation of Islam, 1991).
84. Karenga, *Introduction,* 115.
85 Deborah E. Lipstadt, "Not Facing History: Do's and Don'ts of Teaching the Holocaust." *New Republic,* March 6, 1995, 29.
86. For the concept of "industrial killing," see Omer Bartov, *Murder in Our Midst* (New York: Oxford University Press), 3–10.
87. Every high school student and college freshman should be encouraged to read Seymour Dreschen's cogent and brilliant article "The Atlantic Slave Trade and the Holocaust: A Comparative Analysis," in *Is the Holocaust Unique? Perspectives on Comparative Genocide,* ed. Alan S. Rosenbaum (Boulder: Westview, 1996), 72. See also Laurence Thomas, "American Slavery and the Holocaust: Their Ideologies Compared," in *Subjugation and Bondage,* ed. Tommy L. Lott (Lanham, Md.: Rowman & Littlefield, 1998), 255–278. For a moving depiction of the "Zong affair," see Fred D'Aguiar's novel *Feeding the Ghosts* (London: Vintage, 1997).
88. Dreschen, "The Atlantic Slave Trade and the Holocaust."
89. Wolfgang Sofsky, *The Order of Terror: The Concentration Camp,* trans. William Temple (Princeton: Princeton University Press, 1997), 171. On this point, see also Richard L. Rubenstein, *The Cunning of History* (New York: Harper Colophon, 1978), 41.
90. Sofsky, *The Order of Terror,* 171–172.
91. For scholarly use of the term in regard to the genocide of Native Americans, see David E. Stannard, *American Holocaust: The Conquest of the New World* (New York: Oxford University Press, 1992); Russell Thornton, *American Indian Holocaust and Survival* (Norman: University of Oklahoma Press, 1990), chap. 4. For gays, see Larry Kramer, *Reports From the Holocaust* (New York: St. Martin's, 1994).
92. On this point see Ian Buruma, "The Joys of Victimhood," *New York Review of Books,* April 8, 1999.
93. "The Deforming Mirror of Truth," in *Revelations,* ed. Nathan Huggins (New York: Oxford University Press, 1995), 252–283.
94. John Murray Cuddihy, *The Ordeal of Civility* (New York: Dell, 1974), 210.
95. Ralph A. Austen, "The Uncomfortable Relationship: African Enslave-

ment in the Common History of Blacks and Jews," *Tikkun* 9, no. 2 (1994): 65–68, 86; Martin, *Jewish Onslaught*, 45. For a discussion of Leonard Jeffries's strange construction of the world of race, see Eric Pooley, "The Rise of Afrocentric Conspiracy Theorist Leonard Jeffries and His Odd Ideas about Blacks and Whites," *New York Magazine*, September 2, 1991, 33–37. The phrase "rich Jews" is found on page 33 of Pooley. See also James Traub, *City on a Hill* (Menlo Park: Addison-Wesley, 1994), chap. 13.

96. Quoted in Pooley, "The Rise of Afrocentric Conspiracy Theorist Leonard Jeffries," 33.

97. Clarke, "Black Demagogues and Pseudo-Scholars," in *Black Books Bulletin*, 10.

98. For Jewish responses to the charges that Jews financed and organized the slave trade, see Austen, "Uncomfortable Relationship"; Harold Brackman, *Farrakhan's Reign of Historical Error: The Truth behind the Secret Relationship between Blacks and Jews* (Los Angeles: Simon Wiesenthal Center, 1992); David Brion Davis, *Slavery and Human Progress* (New York: Oxford University Press, 1984), 92; Davis, "The Slave Trade and the Jews," *New York Review of Books*, December 22, 1994, 14–16; Eli Faber, *Jews, Slaves, and the Slave Trade* (New York: New York University Press, 1998); Saul S. Friedman, *Jews and the American Slave Trade* (New Brunswick, N.J.: Transaction, 1998).

99. The literature on West African slavery is voluminous. These three books contain valuable discussions of African participation in the trade: Herbert S. Klein, *The Atlantic Slave Trade* (New York: Cambridge University Press, 1999); Hugh Thomas, *The Slave Trade* (New York: Simon & Schuster, 1997); Joseph C. Miller, *Way of Death* (Madison: University of Wisconsin Press, 1988). For a discussion of Africans' recognition of their complicity in the slave trade, see the *New York Times*, December 27, 1994, A4.

100. Clarke, "Black Demagogues and Pseudo-Scholars," 14.

101. Some would maintain that black anti-Semites' ideas about Jews are no different from those entertained by European anti-Semites and present-day members of the Christian Identity Movement. See Michael Barkun, *Religion and the Racist Right* (Chapel Hill: University of North Carolina Press, 1994).

102. The Jews have been replaced in the inner cities by a new group of so-called exploiters in the form of East Indians and Koreans. For the Koreans, see Itabari Njeri, *The Last Plantation* (Boston: Houghton Mifflin, 1997); and Pyong Gap Min, *Caught in the Middle: Korean Merchants in America's Multiethnic Cities* (Berkeley: University of California Press, 1996).

103. A similar although not identical scapegoating of homosexuals can be found among Asians, Native Americans, and Latinos. For an interesting discussion of homosexuality among what is erroneously referred to as

men of color, see *Men of Color: A Context for Service to Homosexually Active Men*, ed. John F. Longress, Ph.D. (Binghamton, N.Y.: Haworth, 1996). See my review of this book, entitled "Invisible Men," in *Multicultural Education* 5 (Winter 1997): 32–33.

104. Thomas Jefferson, *Notes on the State of Virginia* (1785; reprint, New York: Harper & Row, 1964), 134.

105. Pooley, "The Rise of Afrocentric Conspiracy Theorist Leonard Jeffries," 37.

106. Asante, *Afrocentricity*, 57. See also the bizarre interpretation of black male homosexuality in Dr. Frances Cress Welsing, *The Isis Papers* (Chicago: Third World, 1991), chap. 6. Both the logic and the historical underpinnings of this essay escape me. Kendall Thomas has written a brilliant essay on black homophobia, "Ain' Nothin' Like the Real Thing," in *Representing Black Men*, ed. Marcellus Blount and George P. Cunningham (New York: Routledge, 1996), 55–69. The issue of outsiderness, that is, as gay, not black, is discussed in Cathy Cohen, *The Boundaries of Blackness* (Chicago: University of Chicago Press, 1997).

107. Quoted in Don Belton, "How To Make Love to a White Man," *Transitions* 73, no. 7 (1998): 172.

108. For fascist sexual practice, see the following works: Victoria De Grazia, *How Fascism Ruled Women in Italy, 1922–1945* (Berkeley: University of California Press, 1992); Claudia Koonz, *Mothers in the Fatherland* (New York: St. Martin's, 1986); George L. Mosse, *Nationalism and Sexuality* (New York: Howard Fertig, 1985); Barbara Spackman, *Fascist Virilities* (Minneapolis: University of Minnesota Press, 1996).

109. Eve Lewin, *Sex and Society in the World of the Orthodox Slavs, 900–1700* (Ithaca: Cornell University Press, 1989), 14.

110. Jeffrey Weeks, *Coming Out* (London: Quartet, 1997), 3.

111. Ibid. The creation of modern homosexual identity in America is discussed in George Chauncy, *Gay New York* (New York: Basic, 1994) and John D'Emilio, *Sexual Politics, Sexual Communities: The Making of a Homosexual Minority in the United States, 1940–1970* (Chicago: University of Chicago Press, 1983).

112. The history of homosexuality has blossomed in the last decade and the literature on this subject grows daily. Rudi C. Bleys, *The Geography of Perversion* (New York: New York University Press, 1995); John Boswell, *Christianity, Social Tolerance, and Homosexuality* (Chicago: University of Chicago Press, 1980); Mark Gevisser and Edwin Cameron, eds., *Defiant Desire: Gay and Lesbian Lives in South Africa* (New York: Routledge, 1995); David M. Halperin, *One Hundred Years of Homosexuality* (New York: Routledge, 1990); Gilbert Herdt, *Guardians of the Flutes* (New York: Columbia University Press, 1987); Herdt, *Third Sex, Third Gender* (New York: Zone, 1994); Bert Hinsch, *Passions of the Cut Sleeve: The Male Homosexual Tradition in China* (Berkeley: University of California Press,

1990); Tsueno Watanabe and Jun'ichi Iwata, *The Love of the Samurai: A Thousand Years of Japanese Homosexuality*, trans. D. R. Roberts (London: GMP, 1989); Gary P. Leupp, *Male Colors: The Construction of Homosexuality in Tokugawa Japan* (Berkeley: University of California Press, 1995); Neil Miller, *Out in the World: Gay and Lesbian Life from Buenos Aires to Bangkok* (New York: Vintage, 1992); Stephen O. Murray, *Latin American Male Homosexualities* (Albuquerque: University of New Mexico Press, 1995); Stephen O. Murray and Will Roscoe, *Islamic Homosexualities* (New York: New York University Press, 1997); Murray and Roscoe, *Boy Wives and Female Husbands* (New York: St. Martin's, 1998); Will Roscoe, *The Zuni Man-Woman* (Albuquerque: University of New Mexico Press, 1991); Arno Schmitt and Jehoeda Sofer, eds., *Sexuality and Eroticism among Males in Moslem Societies* (Binghamton, N.Y.: Harrington Park, 1992); Richard C. Trexler, *Sex and Conquest* (Ithaca: Cornell University Press, 1995); Walter L. Williams, *The Spirit and the Flesh* (Boston: Beacon, 1986). *The Lesbian and Gay Studies Reader*, ed. Henry Abelove, Michele A. Barale, and David M. Halprin (New York: Routledge, 1993), is an essential source for the study of lesbian and gay history.

113. Murray and Roscoe use the term "homosexualities" to describe same-sex behavior in Africa: *Boy-Wives*, xviii. For Evans-Pritchard's work, see Edward Evans-Pritchard, "Sexual Inversion among the Azande," *American Anthropologist* 72 (1970): 1428–1434.

114. For the concept of covert categories, see Stephen O. Murray, "The Will Not to Know: Islamic Accommodations of Male Homosexuality," in *Islamic Homosexualities*, ed. Stephen O. Murray and Will Roscoe (New York: New York University Press, 1997), 14–54.

115. Murray and Roscoe, *Boy-Wives*, xii.

116. Ibid.

117. Ibid., xi.

118. For a superb discussion of mulattoes and hybridity, see Robert J. C. Young, *Colonial Desire: Hybridity in Theory, Culture, and Race* (New York: Routledge, 1995), chap. 1.

119. Quoted in the *San Francisco Chronicle*, January 12, 1994, A6.

120. Sister Souljah, *No Disrespect* (New York: Vintage, 1996), 225. For Reggie White's strange opinions about not only homosexuals but also whites, Asians, and Latinos, see *Jet*, April 13, 1998, 55–56.

121. Cornell West, *Race Matters* (Boston: Beacon, 1993), 35.

122. *New York Times Book Review*, January 14, 1996, 9.

123. Molefi K. Asante, "Ancient Africa's Influence," *Emerge*, July–August 1996, 66–69.

124. Nietzsche, "On the Uses and Disadvantages of History for Life," 102.

125. Tom Wolf, *From Bauhaus to Our House* (New York: Farrar Straus Giroux, 1981), 18–19.

126. Bernard Ortiz de Montellano, Gabriel Haslip-Viera, and Warren Barbour,

"They Were NOT Here before Columbus: Afrocentric Hyperdiffusionism in the 1990s," *Ethnohistory* 44 (Spring 1997): 202.

127. Quoted in ibid., 203.
128. Tony Horowitz, *Confederates in the Attic* (New York: Pantheon, 1998).
129. De Montellano, "They Were NOT Here before Columbus," 200.
130. Brent D. Shaw, "A Groom of One's Own," *New Republic*, July 18 and 25, 1994, 40.
131. See Roy Kerridge, *The Story of Black History* (London: Claridge, 1998), for a similar process in Britain.

INDEX